D0983945

ECUMENICAL STUDIES IN WORSHIP

NO. 19

THE LORD'S SUPPER

by

JEAN-JACQUES von ALLMEN
Professor of Practical Theology
in the University of Neuchâtel

JOHN KNOX PRESS
Richmond, Virginia

Library of Congress Catalog Card Number: 76–79925

ECUMENICAL STUDIES IN WORSHIP

General Editors:

J. G. DAVIES, M.A., D.D.
Edward Cadbury Professor of Theology and Director of the Institute for the Study of Worship and Religious Architecture in the University of Birmingham

A. RAYMOND GEORGE, M.A., B.D.
Principal, Richmond College, University of London

Advisory Board:

PROFESSOR J.-J. VON ALLMEN
University of Neuchâtel

PROFESSOR OSCAR CULLMANN
Universities of Basel and Sorbonne

PROFESSOR H. GRADY DAVIS
Chicago Lutheran Seminary

DR. F. W. DILLISTONE
Fellow of Oriel College, Oxford

PROFESSOR ROGER HAZELTON
Andover-Newton Theological Seminary, Mass.

PROFESSOR J. KUMARESAN
Gurukul Lutheran College, Madras

DR. R. STUART LOUDEN
Kirk of the Greyfriars, Edinburgh

PROFESSOR ROBERT NELSON
University of Boston Theological School, Boston, Mass.

CANON D. R. VICARY
Headmaster, King's School, Rochester, England

CONTENTS

COPYRIGHT © 1966 DELACHAUX ET NIESTLÉ S.A., NEUCHÂTEL,
SWITZERLAND

ENGLISH TRANSLATION © 1969 LUTTERWORTH PRESS

This book originally appeared as *Essai sur le Repas du
Seigneur*, *Cahiers Théologiques*, No. 55, Éditions Delachaux et Niestlé, Neuchâtel. The English translation was
done by W. Fletcher Fleet.

LUTTERWORTH PRESS
4 BOUVERIE STREET, LONDON, E.C.4

JOHN KNOX PRESS
RICHMOND, VIRGINIA,

Standard Book Number: 8042-3813-8

Printed in Great Britain

INTRODUCTION

IN 1520, MARTIN LUTHER published *Ein Sermon von dem Neuem Testament, d.i. von der Heiligen Messe*.[1] Thus he established conformity between the Lord's Supper and the New Testament, which is the final word on relations between God and men. This conformity goes back to the most ancient attestation of the institution of the Lord's Supper: "This cup is the new testament in my blood", said Jesus (1 Cor. 11: 25; cf. Luke 22: 20).

When we consider the Eucharist, we are at the very heart of the Gospel and of the life which it creates in the Church. I would go even further and say we are, secretly, at the place and time which have a decisive effect on the life of the world since, through the power of the Holy Spirit, the Supper exemplifies, renews and renders effective the place and the time where the fate and salvation of mankind are enacted. That is why the Supper is a kind of crucible in which all the elements which constitute the Gospel are combined. That is why the Supper—certainly not through the varied theological interpretations given to it but through the reality of its occurrence—remains a mystery to the present world; and it is as the Supper is given its central place in the life of the Church that the Church in her turn is protected against all that would compromise her eschatological nature.

We should, therefore, not be surprised that the Supper, so intimately associated with the Good News incarnate in Jesus of Nazareth, has always been the target of the Adversary. Yet, distorted, amputated, neglected or paralysed, attacked on one side by magic and superstition and by rationalism on the other, the Supper has persisted, not always without difficulty, in enriching the believers and in summoning the Church to celebrate it more reverently and to interpret it more faithfully, more comprehensively and more profoundly. It is not surprising that the Supper should be the final test of peace and unity in the Church or, to express it negatively, that it is over the celebration and interpretation of the Supper that dogmatic and canonical divisions are most evident.

9

"It is the glory of God to conceal a thing", says one of the Proverbs (25: 2). God visited the world incognito in the person of a Jew; He chose the weak and foolish things of the world to confound the strong and wise. But into this weakness and folly He put all His strength and wisdom. The Supper shares to a large degree this choice of weakness and folly. Not only because no liturgy can ever adequately express the eucharistic event, nor yet because a piece of bread can have no visible connection with the flesh given by Jesus for the life of the world, but much more because of the very considerable difficulty there is in following the clues which lead from the Supper celebrated by the Church to the moment when, on the night in which He was betrayed,[2] Jesus instituted the meal which was to bear His name. Indeed it must be admitted, in view of recent researches, that our sources do not enable us to affirm the exact nature of the institution of the Supper or the apostolic way of celebrating (if we can speak of any one way) without running the risk of being contradicted. This impression affects, for example, the following points.

When did Jesus institute the Supper? Was it during the celebration of the Jewish Passover meal? Scholars have multiplied arguments for and against, as if the theological interpretation of the Supper depended entirely on the conclusion reached. Today it seems, however, that at least until new documentary evidence is forthcoming which might allow the debate to be re-opened, a compromise has been reached in which the idea of the paschal setting—whether precisely stated or implied from the context—is inseparable from the institution of the Supper, that undeniably the paschal setting is of major importance for the understanding and assessment of the Supper, but that it is impossible to be more specific.[3]

What were the words spoken by Jesus at the time of the Institution? The four accounts that we have do not absolutely coincide. How did Jesus Himself interpret the bread and the cup (or cups)? Did He or did He not give the order for the repetition of what He did on that occasion, as Luke and Paul alone report? Did He specify what He meant by this new covenant-meal by means of teaching which might have been similar to the teaching on the Bread of Life reported in John 6? Did He sum up its true meaning in a prayer, e.g. the high-priestly prayer reported in John 17?[4] Did He, at that time, speak in Aramaic or solemnly in Hebrew? There are so many questions on which historians hesitate to pronounce.

What part was played, in the structure of the eucharistic celebration of the primitive Church, by the apostles' memory of having eaten regularly, not just with an outstanding rabbi, but—after Peter's confession at Caesarea Philippi—with one whom the Living God had revealed to them as His Son, the Christ? What part also was played by their memory of having eaten and drunk with Him after His resurrection from the dead (Acts 10: 41)? How did it come about that the accounts of such meals take on after Pentecost an almost eucharistic coefficient, so that we are led to suppose that every meal Christians ate together was suggestive of the Lord's Supper? In short, have other elements besides the institution by Jesus on the eve of His crucifixion played a part in the progressive formation of eucharistic liturgies? If the answer is Yes, is it possible to determine them with any degree of precision?

These questions preoccupied scholars thirty or forty years ago. The publication in 1926 of H. Lietzmann's *Messe und Herrenmahl, Eine Studie zur Geschichte der Liturgie* (3rd edition, Berlin, 1955) created a great stir, and led to considerable research. Lietzmann, starting from the different liturgical traditions in the post-apostolic age, postulates two different primitive forms of the Supper: the first without direct connection with the last meal of Jesus, but governed by the memory of meals eaten with Him (this would be the Jerusalemite form which reappeared, *via* the Didache, in the Egyptian tradition); the second governed by the memory of the death of Jesus and linked with His last meal with His followers (this would be the Pauline and Synoptic form which re-appeared in the Hippolytan tradition and gained final acceptance throughout the Church). The first was probably characterized by an unbounded exuberance springing from the thought of the resurrection; the second by an increasingly firm insistence on the death of Christ and consequently on the sacrificial aspect of the commemoration.

Lietzmann's hypothesis may now be regarded as impossible: it rests on far too flimsy a foundation;[5] it makes Paul, who held so firmly to the Jerusalem tradition, contradict himself; nor does it explain how the so-called Egyptian tradition could be so rapidly charged with sacrificial meaning.[6] But it must be admitted that Lietzmann's thesis has led to a deepening of the conviction that "the nucleus of the tradition of the accounts of the institution has preserved in a trustworthy manner what Jesus said on the occasion of the Last Supper" (Jeremias), and that it has shown up clearly the part played in the liturgical development by the memory of meals eaten with Jesus, particularly after the resurrection. It may be possible that in the primitive Church the Supper, according to stresses which could vary from place to place, included at the same time repetition of the Last Supper (this supplied the liturgical schema), memory of meals eaten with the Risen Lord (this supplied the overtones of the celebration), and the presence of this schema and of these overtones at the end of a meal where the appetite could be satisfied.

There is a fourth historical point which raises a problem: the place occupied by the Eucharist in the life of the apostolic Church. We have the four accounts of the Institution (the Fourth Gospel does not record it), what St. Paul says in 1 Cor. 10, a fragment at least (6: 51-58) of the Johannine discourse on the Bread of Life, and a number of probable allusions. That is all. Was this seemingly marginal place of the Supper in primitive Christianity due to the fact that the eucharistic life was indeed marginal, or was it due to a very great reticence when the subject was spoken of, because it was the very heart of the life of the Church and this centrality had to be guarded?

One interpretation would support the thesis of those who claim that the Supper grew in importance in proportion to the growing conviction that the Parousia was not imminent, the Supper becoming a kind of substitute Parousia offered to the Church or invented by her to encourage her to be patient. Here one encounters again the old affirmation of Loisy: Jesus preached the advent of the Kingdom and it was the Church which came. In other words, the Church had to come into being because the Kingdom did not come. Whence little by little emerged the rule of faith, the institutional and traditional ministry, the sacraments, the discipline—in short, "pre-catholicism".

The issue is clearly vital: was the Church, or was she not, a fortuitous expedient which Christians had to make the best of so that the message of Jesus should not be lost? And as this procedure has an almost inherent tendency to smother the message, does not fidelity to the message demand an implied infidelity to the Church, or, at the very least, a constant challenging of the Church to prevent her becoming an end in herself? At first sight it must be admitted that one might put this interpretation on the scarcity of New Testament references to the eucharistic life, but in that case one must also suspect that the institution of the Supper by Christ was unhistorical, for when you reduce it to the bare essentials, it is possible to assert that it was when He instituted the Supper that Jesus instituted the Church.

The other alternative, namely that of a maximum silence dictated by discretion, was defended with a great deal of conviction by J. Jeremias. (*Die Abendmahlsworte Jesu,*[6a] 3 ed., Göttingen, 1960, pp. 118–30). He postulates from the beginnings of the Church a secret discipline or the preludes at least to such a discipline. If some scholars disregard his arguments, others have been convinced with good or ill grace. Ph. H. Menoud observes that if the New Testament witness suggests rather than describes the acts of eucharistic worship, it is "as if the intention was to give hints which the initiated would understand and yet which would veil the heart of the Christian worship from those who were outside."[7]

In my opinion, as soon as one begins to study the matter seriously, abundant indications are forthcoming in support of the latter interpretation. St. Paul would never have written about the Eucharist if the Corinthians had not questioned him on this point. For the same reason his reply, which he admits is incomplete (1 Cor. 11: 34), betrays a developed eucharistic theology which, however, he does not expound.[8] The fact is emphasized that when Jesus instituted the Supper only His disciples were present, and that, out of prudence or fear, Christians met behind closed doors (John 20: 19, 26; Acts 12: 12–14; and Rev. 21: 25, where the announcement is made that in the Kingdom the Church will meet with all the doors open) as in the Parable of the Bridegroom (Matt. 25: 10 cf. Luke 13: 25; and perhaps also Matt. 6: 6). No precise information is given about who presided over the eucharistic meetings. Would not the idea of a secret discipline explain why, some time later, Pliny was able to give so little information about Christian worship?

Although the debate opened by Jeremias is not over, I am driven to think we are so accustomed to a Christianity which is openly acknowledged that we find it difficult to understand the very clear, very precise distinctions which the primitive Church had to draw, for her own safety, between open radiance and the secret source of that radiance. It seems possible to me, then, to argue that if we know so little about the eucharistic life of the apostolic Church, it was not because this was negligible, it was because Christians did not talk about it to those outside, and that they wrote about it as little as possible. Perhaps also this was the reason why the written liturgical sources of the primitive Church are so rare: this rarity could indeed bear witness as much to a liturgical secrecy as to a liberty of liturgical improvisation.

The uncertain nature of our historical information about the origin of the Eucharist should not so disturb the Church as to lead her to discourage historians from pursuing their inquiries. They are indeed dedicating themselves to a task which is indispensable to a religion which affirms that God's salvation, in order to reach men and the world, is involved in history and its ambiguities. The Church has nothing to fear since historical hypotheses put forward by this or that scholar are forthwith submitted to searching critical tests. With the help of those hypotheses which have emerged successfully from these tests, the Church may either reach certainty, or (sometimes simultaneously) be led to the place where it is no longer a question of historical assessment, but of an act of faith.

Morever, just as the hesitations of historians in face of the witness borne to the birth, life, death, resurrection and glorification of Jesus are not intended to throw doubt on the confession of His messiahship, but much rather to make it clear that this confession cannot be other than a confession of faith, so the hesitations of the historians in face of the fragmentary and inexplicit information concerning the original doctrine and celebration of the Supper are not intended to make us despair of ever being able to offer to God the worship He desires. On the contrary, they bear witness to the truth that Christian worship is not an action which man controls for himself but is celebrated in an attitude in which man is stripped of his self-sufficiency and his self-righteousness. The ambiguity of our historical knowledge is not strong enough to check or even to interrupt the growth of a spiritual understanding of the Christian cult and of that which constitutes the central element thereof.

Having called attention to four subjects for inquiry relating to the origin of the Supper, we must turn now to the history of the Eucharist. I intend to deal only with three aspects: the liturgical diversity, the eucharistic vocabulary, and the significance of the Reformation in this history.

It is known that the ancient Church possessed different ritual traditions. Historians group them into certain families, and are at variance among themselves over the number and the "genealogy" of these families. The histories of the Christian cult supply most valuable information. Three things seem to be especially interesting for our purpose. First, this ritual diversity, at least in the early stages, did not compromise the unity of the Church, did not hinder a local Church from acknowledging in another local Church the grace which was the source of her own life, even if this other Church possessed a different liturgical tradition. On the contrary, it enabled each local Christian community through and in its worship (which was, as it claimed to be, "catholic") to confess its true nature before God and before the other Churches. Secondly, this liturgical diversity did not spring from any desire to deliver Christian worship from a certain liturgical monotony; different liturgies were not found in each local Church; there were different liturgies because there were different centres of Christian life, local but not yet "confessional". Thirdly, this ancient ritual diversity was gradually reduced to the two liturgies which can be called major: that referred to as the Liturgy of Saint Chrysostom or the Liturgy of Byzantium, and that of Rome.[9] This progressive reduction to two liturgies is due not only to their theological and ritual quality, but also to the political and cultural pre-eminence of Byzantium and Rome and also—for Rome in any case—to certain theological presuppositions regarding the structure of the Church's unity.

For this reason the liturgical tradition which was shaped, stylized and supplied with rubrics at Rome is found just as it is, including the liturgical language, throughout the whole of the West, whereas, by and large,[10] the Byzantine liturgy was celebrated in the everyday language of the people. This reduction of liturgical variation within the "Catholic" Church led, not only to a strong sense of unity and solidarity, but also to a heightening of the tension and to the eventual separation between Rome and Byzantium, as well as to a liturgical revolt against Roman uniformity, even though the great Christian liturgical tradition was more highly valued by the Churches which came under the impact of the Reformation than has sometimes been thought, and not only by Lutherans and Anglicans but even by Calvinists.

The second aspect of the history of the Supper to which I wish to refer concerns eucharistic vocabulary. The striking thing is the astonishing terminological variety in the ancient Church and her apparent refusal to apply doctrinal tests to this vocabulary. It was as though the Christians realized that they could only use faltering words to describe the eucharistic happening. It was as though, when they realized that they had, nevertheless, to make the mystery of the Supper intelligible, they hesitated to make a choice of doctrinal terminology which might lead to the belief that the theologians had solved the mystery. Whence the parallelism between realism, symbolism and spirituality, and the blend of all these which is so surprising in patristic literature, and which enabled those who, in the sixteenth century and later, quoted the Fathers in support of contending views to do so with full justification. But it was realized at that time how rich in meaning the Supper is, so abounding in grace that its very nature was threatened when it was interpreted in a single and exclusive way. In the Corinthian Church it was at the time of the Eucharist that outbreaks of glossolalia occurred. It is quite possible that the terminological profusion which surrounds the Eucharist, which may seem so contradictory, is really a form of glossolalia: a speaking in tongues, interpreted but not edited, for the edification of the Church.

What must also be borne in mind is that during the first millennium the Church experienced no violent controversies or notable heresies concerning the Eucharist. Because of the profoundly grateful emotions which the eucharistic event aroused, the truth concerning the Supper was not, at that time, felt to be cramping and restricting. There was, therefore, no need for anyone to quarrel with the formulation which the Church made in her practice and doctrine of the Eucharist, as there was to be with the dangerous or adulterated formulations of the doctrines of God and of Christ. All this clearly emerges from a rapid and superficial view. If one were to look more closely one would be aware of nuances, inflections, of the direct impact of the great christological or trinitarian conflicts on the doctrine and the celebration of the Eucharist. But actually these are discernible even from far off, as the bitterness of the eucharistic controversies of the sixteenth century may be seen in the background. Whereas in the first millennium close and detailed study has to be made if the internal polemic between the widely different elements which exist side by side in the Supper is to be discerned.

It is indeed astonishing, when you observe the altercations on this theme which resulted from the schisms of the eleventh and sixteenth centuries, that the Church of the first millennium did not seem to take into account the specific and divisive significance of the formal inclusion or omission of an epiklesis, for example, or the all-important bearing of a sacrificial interpretation of the Eucharist, or of a celebration of the Lord's real presence in ill-considered words. It was *a posteriori*, after the division of the Church, that these aspects became subjects for dissension. Why? Perhaps because the Supper fits ill into a divided Church, since division calls into question one of its special purposes: unity. Perhaps, too, because Christian disunity threatens to isolate one particular element of the eucharistic life and make it distorted or heretical, not intrinsically, but because this particular element can no longer be completed or balanced by other elements in this life.

If almost all the western distortions of the Supper are found, often in a very vigorous form, before the eleventh century, if the eucharistic theology, practice and devotion of the West in the Middle Ages can on the whole claim to find their origins at least in earlier tradition, and if it was only when we became aware of the division which separated us from the East that these elements began to appear false in our eyes, then it was disunity which robbed the West of the balance and completeness which safeguarded these traditional elements from pride and self-sufficiency and which allowed them to develop in their own way—bringing about, in the sixteenth century, but within the same distorted frame, the attempt to correct and reform them. The lesson to be drawn from this is so simple as to be suspect. I wonder, however, if it is not true that eucharistic theology, without prejudicing the resolute intention of obeying Christ's intention and the words He spoke at the Institution, is a theology of complementary rather than contradictory alternatives and even a synthesis of elements so diverse that if they became mutually exclusive they would threaten the Christian Supper with dire peril.

The final aspect of the history of the Supper, which I regard as the most important, relates to the Reformation: not so much the profound disagreements which characterized the non-Roman eucharistic theologies when they lost the unity that had been theirs when they were joined in condemnation of the Roman Mass; not so much the recovery of the right to possess different liturgies and consequently the effective discovery, translated into historical facts, that the authentic unity of the Church is not experienced on the ceremonial level. No, what was most important for the history of the Supper at that time was that for the first time men dared to separate the Lord's Day and the Lord's Supper.

The completeness, regularity and speed with which this separation was carried out varied from country to country and from one confession to another; but, if I understand correctly, it happened wherever the Reformation took root. What motivated this separation was the clash between the theological conviction that a eucharistic celebration without the baptized people communicating undergoes a radical change of character and becomes totally unreal, and the pastoral conviction that for the time it was not possible to give communion every Sunday to a laity which, almost in its entirety, had acquired the habit of communicating only once a year, at Easter. They therefore took the risk of celebrating the Supper no longer every Sunday, but as often as was pastorally possible, and at least on the major festivals, in the hope that the frequency of celebration would increase. We know now that this hope was not fulfilled in the Reformed Churches on the Continent and for almost three centuries in the Church of England.

Now this divorce between the Lord's Day and the Lord's Supper, and the consequent possibility of thereafter celebrating the Lord's Day without also celebrating the Supper which He had instituted for that day, without doubt divided the Church more radically than any of the previous schisms, at least as far as the people of the Church were aware. This divorce has led to the emergence of two types of Christianity: the "Catholic" type which has maintained the hitherto unanimous tradition (even if, in certain areas, an equivocal and heretical tradition), and the "Protestant" type which has produced a *sentire ecclesiam*, a religious sociology, movements of ideas which do not necessarily exclude the sacramental life but remain on the fringe of it.

The result is that the sociological affinities between "Protestant" churches are felt to be stronger links than the theological affinity between any one "Protestant" Church and "Catholic" tradition, for the division in Christendom is not only an object of study for theologians, a source of pride or of shame to the leaders of the Church, a source of scandal to the world, but also, and especially since the sixteenth century, an element which is frighteningly real in the reflexes and in the life of Christian people.

If it was difficult in former days to heal schisms between churches whose people, once passions were no longer enflamed, succeeded without too much difficulty in rediscovering the source of their life and joy in the Church with whom reconciliation had to be made, it is much more difficult today to envisage and to work for a union between churches whose members have the utmost difficulty in acknowledging, on the surface or in depth, their own church life in the life of the other.

To reach a worthy understanding of the holy Supper, mention must be made of the method which will be followed. The Eucharist— like Christology, the supreme theological study—demands a way of approach and an exposition which are normative for all theology. This method must follow these rules.

First, it must be bold, and not shrink from the object of study on the grounds that the theme is too rich, too vast or too difficult. It is right and proper that he who knows that he should love God not only with all his heart and strength and soul, but with all his mind, should strive to understand the real nature of the Supper and of what takes place therein. A theology of the Eucharist is an integral part of of the "doctrinal programme" of the Christian Church. The mystery surrounding the Supper neither excludes nor condemns the searching consideration, critical, free, and enthusiastic of the scholar who is involved in the eucharistic life of the Church.

In the second place, this method must be ecclesial and biblical or biblical and ecclesial, the order of the words being reversible since they can be taken as having the same meaning. It must be ecclesial because (again as in the case of Christology to which eucharistic theology is so closely related—and for a very good reason) faith is necessary, so that the eyes may see and the ears hear what is happening at the holy Supper. Apart from the Church, from the desire to be part of the Church, from conscious awareness of being in the Church, reflection on the Eucharist would be deprived of one of its essential references, since there is no Supper apart from the Church, and no Church apart from the Supper, since it is impossible to isolate the Supper from the Church which finds her foundation and her fulfil-ment in the Supper. This way of approach and exposition is ecclesial, but with overtones of criticism; that is to say, it is biblical. It is set within the limits measured out by the unanimous consent of the ancient Church so that the faith, worship and discipline of the Church might be planted and grow in liberty and obedience. In other words, the attainments of the post-apostolic theological traditions do not demand a restrictive and uniform approach, but, on the contrary, they may be re-examined with reference to the New Testament standard, which in particular will enable the Church to be freed from certain narrow interpretations, over-emphases, or fears which might be dominant at certain periods, but which might distort the very object being studied if treated as indispensable and integral elements of the Supper.

Finally, this method must be communicable, not possessive. The Eucharist is not a prize to be grasped, or a mechanism to be dismantled. It has been properly called a mystery. Balaam, constrained to bless Israel, however unwilling he was, spoke about himself words which ought to be the motto of every theologian "who sees the vision of the Almighty falling down" (Num. 24: 4, 16).[11]

A theologian is one who knows how to pray is the assertion of the Eastern tradition, according to Gregory of Nyssa and Evagrius Ponticus. προσφορά, ἀναφορά, oblatio are words which have played a considerable part in the history of the Eucharist. Their real meaning and their *raison d'être* are found if they also express the right approach to the understanding of the Eucharist. It is not a question of renouncing reason when confronted by the Supper. Rather it is a question of not trying to monopolize—in order to dismantle and reassemble it as though it were a gadget—the event which brings it about that, when one eats of this bread and drinks of this cup, one's soul and body are nourished for eternal life, because this bread is the body of Christ and the cup is the new covenant in His blood.

When Moses, initiated into the art of magic through his Egyptian education, wished to walk around the burning bush to find out the cause of this amazing phenomenon that he could see there, he was rebuked: this bush which bore within itself a fire which needed no fuel, this bush whose wood resisted the fire which dwelt within the wood but did not succeed in burning it up, this fire-wood, this wood-fire united for a single epiphany and yet distinct from each other, without confusion, without division and without separation of its essential emphases, was not an object of curiosity, but an invitation to adoration (Exod. 3: 2 ff.). It is in this attitude that eucharistic theology is to be approached.

The Eucharist is not an object, it is a way of life. For this reason we shall endeavour to consider its living character by the method of approach and exposition. Now life is full of tensions, of polarities, of complements between which the balance has to be maintained. Learning from the ancient Church, but for the benefit of the Church today, we shall endeavour to imply the very special character of the subject awaiting our study by the manner in which we treat it. Yngve Brilioth saw in the Eucharist five major emphases: the act of thanksgiving, the communion, the commemoration, the sacrifice and the mystery; and he observed rightly that if any of these emphases is given more prominence than another, the Supper itself is endangered.[12] I should like to widen a little this approach to the eucharistic question and look at the Supper from six different aspects. I particularly wish to emphasize that each one of these aspects is doubly polarized, and that this series of double polarizations, through the tensions which it suggests, offers precisely the road to an interpretation of the Lord's Supper which is at the same time bold, biblical, ecclesial, and communicable.

We shall begin by looking at the Supper as a memorial of the history of salvation and of participation in this history through the power of the Holy Spirit (Chap. I). This will be followed by an examination of the ecclesiological character of the Supper from the strictly ecclesiological angle (Chap II. The Supper as revelation of the limitations and fulfilment of the Church) and the communal aspect (Chap. III). Then we shall have to face the most delicate feature of eucharistic theology: the moment when the gift of grace and the offering of thanksgiving meet (Chap. IV). The two aspects of the eucharistic life which remain are: the Supper as the focus where, here below, the prayer of the Church and the fulfilment of this prayer meet (Chap. V), and the Supper as the place where the very life of the Church in the world pulsates, as the place where the Church is sent into the world to fulfil her apostolic ministry, the place whither she returns from the world to offer her worship (Chap. VI).

This ambivalence of the Supper will not be treated *in extenso*. I shall fix a few guide marks which will enable those who read right to the end to taste and see how gracious the Lord is.

NOTES

[1] *Luthers Werke in Auswahl*, ed. O. Clemen, vol. I, Berlin, 1933, pp. 299–322.

[2] Lacking the most elementary competence, I am leaving aside the problem of the textual variants in Luke's Gospel concerning the institution of the Supper. One can find all the relevant information in the works on the origin of the Eucharist and in the commentaries. I note simply that the text called "long" (because it does not omit chapter 22, verses 19b–20) is more and more recognized as the most reliable, not only because it is better attested, but because no other source gives us a Eucharist which follows the order, cup—bread, rather than bread—cup (1 Cor. 10: 16, 21 is irrelevant here as Paul in 1 Cor. 11: 23 ff. recounts the institution of the Supper in the normal order). I am of the opinion that we must conclude with A. J. B. Higgins, *The Lord's Supper in the New Testament*, Studies in Biblical Theology, 6, London, 1964, p. 40, that the first cup, which was not linked with the blood of the new covenant, "was not regarded as an eucharistic cup".

[3] The thesis of Théo Preiss, according to which there is more support for the idea of a paschal *setting* than for a precise paschal chronology, is gaining more followers.

[4] R. Bultmann (*Das Evangelium des Johannes* 1954–56, p. 371) is of the opinion that the author of the Fourth Gospel inserted this prayer "in the place of the Lord's Supper . . . and clearly with unmistakable reference to the Sacrament of the Eucharist".

[5] Viz. the transposition of Did. 10: 6 and Did. 9: 1–10: 5 which would permit the interpretation of the latter text as referring not to the Agape which precedes the Eucharist, but as the Eucharist itself. J. Jeremias, by this argument, dismantled Lietzmann's theory. (*op. cit.*, p. 127, note 7.)

[6] Two other hypotheses concerning the origin of the Christian Supper were long debated, but now seem to be discarded: one looked for it in meals commemorating the dead in the Hellenistic world (but Jesus did not stay in the world of the dead!); the other sought it in the Hellenistic mysteries (but what the Supper celebrates is linked not to myths but to an historic event!).

[6a] Eng. Tr. *The Eucharistic Words of Jesus*, London, 1966.

[7] *La vie de l'Eglise naissante*, Neuchâtel and Paris, 1952, p. 36; cf. p. 39.

[8] P. Neuenzeit rightly insists on the fact that the frequency of eucharistic celebration must have contributed quite early to the elaboration of a profound eucharistic theology, *Das Herrenmahl, Studien zur Paulinischen Abendsmahlsauffassung*, Munich, 1960, p. 238.

[9] All diversity has not been stifled. In the Orthodox Churches, the so-called Liturgy of St. Basil, once a "major" liturgy, is still celebrated ten times a year. Also in the West, certain local Churches and religious orders retain, as somewhat of a privilege, the right to certain liturgical peculiarities. And if other ancient liturgical traditions have remained alive, it is thanks to the Monophysites or Nestorians.

[10] I am referring not so much to the language used in Slavonic countries for the celebration of the liturgy, which is no longer that of everyday speech; I would rather call attention to a coincidence which merits serious study: the disappearance of the Church, under the pressure of Islam, in the territories where the liturgical language was not the language (or dialect) of the people, whether in North Africa or in the hinterland of Asia Minor.

[11] I am aware that the verb *napal* has other meanings besides "to prostrate oneself" (cf., however, Gen. 17: 3; 44: 14; 2 Sam. 1: 2; Job 1: 20) e.g. "fall into an ecstasy", or as *LXX* translates it, "to be $\dot{\epsilon}\nu$ $\ddot{\upsilon}\pi\nu\omega$.

[12] *Eucharistic Faith & Practice, Evangelical and Catholic*, London, 1956, p. 48.

I

ANAMNESIS AND EPIKLESIS

ATTEMPTS HAVE OFTEN been made to interpret the Supper in the light
of the Greek mysteries, and it would be idle to deny that there is a
certain superficial kinship between the Greek mystery-cult and the
Christian Supper. There is, however, an essential and radical difference:
the Christian Supper offers to those who participate in it, not the experience of being in communion with a myth, but participation in
historical events. That is what is meant by anamnesis: the possibility
of participating in the history which is being recalled and, in principle,
this affirmation might be adequate to define and describe the Christian
Supper. We shall see that if it is inadequate, it is because this affirmation is threatened from two sides. There is first the danger of reading
into the anamnesis a certain automatic efficacy, and then the danger, as a
reaction, of depriving the anamnesis of its power of communication.

The Church did not invent the Supper. It is the last thing the Church
could have invented. For the Church, the celebration of the Supper
is obedience to an order of Christ, as the celebration of the Passover
was for Israel an act of obedience to the order of God: "Do this in
remembrance of me" (1 Cor. 11: 24 ff.; Luke 22: 19; cf. Exod. 12–13).
The Supper is thus the worship which Jesus Christ instituted for the
New People who find in Him the ground of their existence and their
life. There is something very striking in that: Jesus did not institute a
festival (in the Hebrew anamnetic sense of the term) intended to
celebrate henceforth a fresh work of God; He turned what He Himself
had done into a festival, which implies that it was indeed Jesus who
instituted the Supper (and the accounts of the institution, despite the
problems they raise, have stood up against the doubts of scholars,
whether or not these doubts are "occupational"). He attributed to
His death a vital significance for the world's salvation, He made it
the foundation of a New Covenant.

But what is the meaning of anamnesis, the Hebrew *zikārōn* which is
so difficult to translate exactly: memory, memorial, celebration, or

cultic commemoration? Researches pursued during recent decades have led to a certain consensus of opinion; anamnesis, in the meaning which interests us in this study, is the ritual recalling of a past event to restore its original virtue and, even more, the setting of those who engage in the anamnesis in the very event which the celebration commemorates. Reference may be made to the saying of Gamaliel when expounding, in the light of Exod. 13:8, the event of the Israelite Passover: "Every man in every generation must consider himself as having been personally delivered from Egypt. Every Israelite must know that he personally has been freed from slavery."[1] The anamnesis is therefore much more than a mnemonic ceremony; it is a re-enactment of the event which the celebration commemorates.

This interpretation of the anamnesis is of paramount importance. It offers a way of escape from the dilemma of unacceptable alternatives. It enables us to understand why the early Church, whose very life it constituted, did not experience the conflicts over this issue which, later, rent the Western Church. This interpretation of the anamnesis compromises neither the uniqueness nor the sufficiency of the death of Christ. In consequence, it avoids a doctrine of the Eucharist which sees in the Supper a repetition of Calvary which is necessary if the death of Christ is not to lose its saving power. But, on the other hand, this interpretation of the anamnesis does not downgrade the celebration of the Supper into a mere "memorial meal" which would have little more than a psychological or sentimental significance, totally unrelated to those who take part in it and making it optional, with no justification for its necessity except by recourse to the command of Christ, a command which is odd and perhaps even unhistorical. Therefore this interpretation respects what F. J. Leenhardt had the courage to call "the efficacy of the rite."[2] It then becomes possible to speak of the saving significance of the Supper without doing despite to the uniqueness and sufficiency of the death of Christ. It is possible also to insist on this sufficiency and this uniqueness without the Supper becoming superfluous. With this in mind, we must see what event the anamnesis celebrates and before whom it is carried out.

significance

The Supper is the anamnesis of Jesus (εἰς τὴν ἐμὴν ἀνάμνησιν). This is very significant, as the accounts of the Institution and the Pauline affirmation that the Lord's death is proclaimed (1 Cor. 11:26) in the Supper point out the anamnesis is primarily of the Cross. One thing, however, is significant: from the beginning the anamnesis of this death

24

was deliberately celebrated on Sundays and not on Fridays when the actual event took place (cf. Acts 20: 7). This was because, in the New Testament situation, it was impossible to commemorate the death of Jesus without commemorating His resurrection also, or without commemorating His death in the light of His resurrection. The so-called Liturgy of Saint Basil is perfectly loyal to the New Testament when, at the time of the Institution, it puts into Christ's mouth the words: "Each time that you eat this bread and drink this cup, you proclaim my death and *bear witness to my resurrection.*" But that is not all: the cross and the resurrection cannot be wrested from their context. For this reason, when the death and resurrection are remembered, the whole life of Jesus has to be brought into the commemoration, to be proclaimed, to be solemnly "attested", as the Gallican liturgies expressed it. The following passage, for example, is found in the eucharistic prayer in *The Apostolic Tradition* of Hippolytus of Rome:

> We give thanks to Thee, O God, for Thy well-beloved servant Jesus Christ, whom Thou hast sent in these latter days to be our saviour, redeemer and the messenger of Thy will; for Him who is the Word, inseparable from Thee, by whom Thou hast made all things and in whom Thou hast delighted; Thou didst send Him from heaven into a virgin's womb: being conceived in her womb, He was incarnate and manifested as Thy Son, born of the Holy Spirit and of the Virgin; to fulfil Thy will and to gain for Thee a holy people, He stretched forth His hands in His agony to deliver from suffering those who believe on Thee. When of His own free will He was delivered up to suffering to rob death of his power, to break Satan's bonds, to trample on hell, to illuminate the righteous, to consolidate the frontier, to bring immortality to light, having taken the bread and giving thanks to Thee, He said: Take, eat, this is my body which is broken for you.

But this retrospective résumé of the life of Christ is not sufficient for the memorial. The Easter victory is so sovereign that in consequence of it the Parousia can already be celebrated:

> Remembering, therefore, the beneficial commandment and all that has been accomplished for us: His cross, His burial, His resurrection on the third day, His ascension into heaven, His presence at the right hand of the Father, *His second and glorious coming.*[3]

So, little by little, the Church came to understand that, in the thirty or so hours between the death and resurrection of Jesus, the true interpretation of the world and its history became apparent. For this reason, as in olden days around Noah's Ark, all whom Christ came to die for, all who in Him desire to escape the judgment of God, gather now around the memorial of the Cross.

My mind turns, for example, to the magnificent preface to the *Apostolic Constitutions* where, before the anamnesis properly speaking comes, there is a kind of fresh convocation of creation and history around Him who created everything in heaven and on earth. (Col. 1: 16.)

So, because the Cross can never be isolated from that for which it was erected, since it is at the same time the key to and the culminating point in the history of salvation, the anamnesis of the death of Christ implies, explicitly or implicitly, the anamnesis of the entire history of salvation, (whence the *memento* of those who already rest in Christ as well as of those alive today who bear the marks of the suffering and the glory of Christ; whence, also, the concern of the eucharistic litanies for the world and what is happening in it). Since it is an anamnesis of the death of Christ, the Supper links salvation to history and at the same time casts on to this history the light which enables us to understand it.

It is at this point that we must speak of the relation between the eucharistic celebration and the ministry of the Word in the worship of the Church.[4]

Briefly, two observations have to be made. The first is so obvious that it is hardly necessary to make it: the Supper is celebrated with the aid of speech; it is not mimed. What Jesus did on the night when He was betrayed is recalled, the words He pronounced over the bread and the cup are repeated, it is affirmed that the broken bread is communion in His body and the cup of blessing communion in His blood (1 Cor. 10: 16 ff.), prayers are offered, hymns are sung. It is quite possible that, from the very beginning, the Supper was accompanied by a eucharistic catechesis of which John 6: 51c–58 may be an example.[5] The Word is essential to an understanding of the Supper. The liturgical action is celebrated explicitly, in such a way as to be understood. That is why it is somewhat of a slight on the baptized who are taking part in the worship when the clergy conduct the liturgy in a language other than that spoken by the congregation, or when, for certain prayers, the celebrant lowers his voice to a whisper, as if only the clergy formed the Church, as if they had to resort to a secret code to protect themselves from the world represented by the laity.

But if the Word is essential to the understanding of the Supper, the Supper is equally essential to the understanding of the Word, which the Supper explains and illumines in two special directions. First, it takes away the veil which covers the eyes of the Jews when they read the Old Testament (cf. 2 Cor. 3: 14), since it is only after the inauguration of the New Covenant, the Covenant of the Spirit (2 Cor. 3: 6), that the Old Testament yields its secret. It is not an exaggeration to say that the Supper, for Christians and Jews alike, supplies the authentic key to the interpretation of the Old Testament. This is the meaning of the story which tells how Jesus made Himself known to the disciples at Emmaus. When they saw Him break the bread and at once recognized Him, all that He had expounded to them on the road "beginning with Moses and all the prophets" became at once clear and true (Luke 24: 25-32; 41-47): this suffering was necessary to the world's salvation. This is why the reading of the Old Testament is so important. It keeps alive in the Church the knowledge that salvation is essentially linked with history; it keeps alive the knowledge that the Kingdom, though present already in the Church, is not yet manifest, and that Christians cannot yet enjoy this privilege unequivocally.

The Supper is also of primary importance for the understanding of the word of prophecy in the New Covenant because it reminds us that the true pattern, the true criterion and the true source of any contemporary intervention of God, is the passion and victory of His Son (cf. e.g. 2 Cor. 1: 4 ff.; 10 ff., etc.) and because it enables us to test the spirit of the prophets in order to discern whether they are true or false. Preaching in which the Supper is superfluous, of no practical value or embarrassing, is preaching which leads the Church astray instead of edifying her. This does not mean that the Supper will make the Sunday readings and preaching repetitive and monotonous. Since the Supper constitutes an anamnesis of the event in which the entire history of salvation is concentrated and focused, it enriches and safeguards the ministry of the Word, both read and preached, by supplying its basic hermeneutical principle. Since the Eucharist is the anamnesis of the culminating moment in the history of salvation, it recapitulates in some way the events which prepared the way for the Gospel and brought it into being, as well as the results which have flowed from the Gospel right up to the present day and which will flow from it in the future. Within the Church, in short, there is no need to say anything beyond what is being enacted in the Supper. The same applies to the mission to the world; the Church has nothing to say other than what can find its inspiration or confirmation in the Supper.

If the anamnesis recalls the history of salvation accomplished in Jesus Christ betrayed for our offences and raised for our justification, who is it who recalls this achievement? At first glance, the reply is obvious: those who perform the anamnesis, namely, the faithful who are celebrating the cult. Through this celebration they claim the benefits of what Christ did once for all, they take their place therein, and the history of salvation, of which they are commemorating the crowning moment, becomes the history of their own salvation.

It is in this sense that the ancient liturgical tradition seems to have understood it. The Greek liturgies regularly say that when the faithful offer to God the eucharistic elements μεμνημένοι, they remember what God did for them and for the world in Jesus Christ. *Ergo memores*, *unde et memores*, or simply *memores*, is what the Latin liturgies generally say. In the liturgies called Gallican are found, with the same meaning, formulae such as: *haec facimus . . . commemorantes et celebrantes passionem unici filii Jesu Christi*. When Justin spoke of the Supper, he said "we always remind each other of these things". It seems then that the anamnesis of the cross, through the Supper, is one of the means instituted by Christ so that those who engage in this anamnesis may thereby be linked with what it commemorates: it enables, therefore, those who carry out this action to "remember", in the sense of participation and identification.

J. Jeremias has put forward an altogether different and carefully documented interpretation: the Church at the time of the Eucharist reminds *God* of the work of the Messiah, so that He may give the signal for the breaking-in of His Kingdom.[6] After shewing that the Eucharist could not even remotely be connected with the funerary memorial meals familiar to the Greeks, since the documents on which they are founded do not include the order for the repetition εἰς ἀνάμνησιν, Jeremias stresses the fact that LXX often uses this Greek phrase with the meaning of a memorial observed so that God may remember and act (cf. Lev. 24: 7; Num. 10: 10, etc.). It is well known that, when God remembers, things happen (Luke 1: 72; Rev. 18: 5)! The Eucharist in this view is an appeal addressed to God to accomplish what the sacrifice of His Son had made possible: the coming of the Kingdom with salvation, not vengeance.

The anamnesis being directed towards God becomes the point at which the Supper reaches at one and the same time its profoundest epikletic intensity and its most potent sacrificial significance: when the Church offers to God in the broken bread and in the cup of the New

Covenant the very symbols of Christ's sacrifice, she is then supplicating God to bring about the indisputable manifestation of the cosmic reconciliation wrought by Christ. When she tries to do this she is, in a way, "plugging in" to this sacrifice for the source of her life. At least these seem to me to be the theological implications of the thesis of J. Jeremias.

This hypothesis "makes one think", as P. Benoit said, although he did not accept it.[7] Indeed it is dismissed, sometimes regretfully, by the majority of specialists in the history of early Christianity, and this rejection must probably be accepted, unless, as proposed by Alan Richardson, it is possible to integrate it into a more comprehensive interpretation of the Supper. What seems to me to undermine the thesis of Jeremias is that, on the one hand, it has no support in the ancient liturgical tradition, and, on the other hand, Jeremias has recourse, to prove his thesis, to a line of argument which destroys the generally accepted meaning of the term anamnesis: in his view, anamnesis can have no other meaning than that of an appeal to God to bring about that for which His Son died, salvation, or else simply an effort of memory on the part of the disciples so that they will not forget Jesus. Even if it is clear that the Church carries out this anamnesis before God, it remains true that it is the Church which remembers: that is to say, that in the Supper the Church is celebrating a memorial of the Passion, instituted by Christ, so that through this memorial she may renew and deepen her integration into the history of salvation, the crowning moment of which is re-enacted in this very memorial. For this reason it should be sufficient, in short, to state that the Supper is an anamnesis of the passion of Jesus Christ.

It must be recognized, however, that the anamnesis, as thus explained, is in danger of being celebrated without due respect and falling into a "eucharistic abuse", either by integrating into the history of salvation persons (and things) which have not passed the strict test of Christian baptism, and so profaning the salvation identified with the eucharistic celebration; or else by manipulating the Supper to appear to control the mystery instead of humbly approaching its service. A protective correction of the anamnesis is thus desirable so that the anamnesis shall not be altered.

A priori, it is possible to conceive of two main types of protective correction (to which the Church adds her discipline in the matter of presiding over the Eucharist); or else it will be said that the saving

realism which we have observed in the anamnesis need not be acknowledged, that the Supper, being only anamnetic, does not give one
a share in the history of salvation, that the Supper has, in short, no
saving significance, that it is a memorial only in the superficial, banal
sense of the term: a memento. In these conditions the danger of a
eucharistic abuse is removed by a kind of castration of the Eucharist
itself: one can no longer understand why Jesus instituted it, nor why
it was not possible to find some better way of performing this exercise
of memorizing the history of salvation, nor why those who do remember cannot do without the Supper. The Supper then is in danger
of becoming a sort of erratic block in the life of the Church which one
occasionally encounters in liturgical traditionalism but which is, in
brief, more of an obstacle than a necessity.

It would be too easy to say that this was the corrective applied by
Zwingli to an anamnetic view of the Supper which bordered on magic.
To single out his conception of the anamnesis does not do justice to
Zwingli's eucharistic theology, which culminates in the affirmation that
the Supper brings the Church into being by transforming her into the
Body of Christ. It must be stated that this way of looking at the
Supper is to be found in wide areas of Protestantism: reduced to a
memorial which has no integral unity with the event which it com-
memorates; it is a source of embarrassment rather than of joy to the
Church.

The other type of protective correction in no sense weakens the
power of the anamnesis, but protects it against the danger of its being
turned in upon itself by the idea that it is offered explicitly to God so
that *He* controls its δύναμις. It is from this perspective that I should
like to understand the epiklesis.

By epiklesis is meant the prayer which calls on the Holy Spirit to
act so that the Supper really becomes what Jesus Christ intended when
He instituted it. It thus seems to raise no particularly delicate problems,
and indeed it does not seem to have raised any as long as it represented
one or other of the liturgical traditions within the united Church.
After the Eastern Schism the question became aggravated and com-
plicated, because the presence or attenuation, if not the complete
absence, of an explicit eucharistic epiklesis coloured the polemic
between the Eastern and Western Churches, or, more likely, because
the attenuation, if not the complete absence, in the West of an explicit
epiklesis where it occurs in the great liturgical tradition of the East
was a fundamental reason for the Eastern Churches' polemic against

Rome. The corollary was that Rome was surprised and somewhat irritated, as she did not infer from this omission what the East inferred. It is a difficult problem. It deserves a detailed study of liturgical history and of comparative liturgiology which is beyond my powers. I will content myself by setting the subject in its theological context, even though this may seem too narrow a view for the experts.

Jesus concluded the discourse in which He had offered eternal life to those who eat His flesh and drink His blood with the words: "It is the Spirit that gives life, the flesh is of no avail" (John 6: 63). This utterance reminds us in the most forceful terms that the mystery and the energy of the Eucharist are not at man's disposal, but must be sought in prayer. The life-giving Spirit is not something to be seized but something bestowed. Simon Magus learnt this to his cost in an exemplary way (Acts 8: 14-24). The Spirit is the first thing for which the Christian must pray.[8]

Was this epikletic prayer in existence in the first apostolic generation? And if so, in what form? The historians have yet to agree on this. What seems certain to me is—whether one concludes that the invocation of the Spirit formed part of the oldest liturgical tradition or not—that it was widespread during the most creative period of liturgical formulation. After that, it was retained in the East, whereas in the West all the evidence points to an increasing neglect of this tradition, either because it was thought that the eucharistic action as a whole was epikletic and that an explicit epiklesis would interrupt the harmony and the logic of the cultic pattern, or because of a progressive distortion of the very theology of the Supper, or, as seems to me most likely, because of a combination of these two reasons.

Perhaps, too, the form of this epiklesis was at first less important than the attitude and impulse which it imposed on the Church. This would enable us to see in the *Maranatha*, which goes back beyond any doubt to the most ancient eucharistic tradition (1 Cor. 16: 22; Did. 10: 6; cf. Rev. 22: 20), an original form of the epiklesis, and would enable us consequently to state that the Eucharist, according to the oldest Christian tradition, makes the Church essentially a praying rather than a triumphant society. We would link this to what we said earlier about the attitude of Moses when he saw the burning bush. This prayerful attitude does not prevent the Church from experiencing, in rich measure, the fulfilment of her prayers. My final chapter will be devoted to this subject.

The epiklesis is, however, more than an attitude. It has, in the ordinary liturgical tradition, a very precise theological connotation. The most common schema is: the Church asks God to send down the Holy Spirit on the congregation and on the eucharistic elements so that they may be consecrated to become the body and blood of Christ and that the congregation may be formed into the one Church and delivered from condemnation at the Last Judgment.

When we try to gather together what the Church then prays for, two things must be emphasized. The Church first beseeches God to renew the event of Pentecost by freely offering to Him the purposes for which this eschatological event is above all desired; the people assembled to commemorate the history of salvation and the bread and wine brought by the Church because those were the elements of the meal which the Lord chose. In other words, the Church shows herself and her gifts, as an offering, so that, because of them, Pentecost may be renewed and remain a living experience, so that the eschatological condition, into which the members of the Church were initiated by baptism, may be confirmed, and that, in this condition, the recapitulation of all things in Christ may be lived out by those who take part in the cult.

In the second place, this oblative prayer is supported by the certainty of its fulfilment. (Did not Jesus promise that God would give the Spirit to those who asked for it? Luke 11: 13.) The Church prays for the coming, not of a pedlar of dreams, but of the πνεῦμα ζωοποιοῦν, the Spirit which has power to confer eternal life, and to transform into eternal truth what is offered in blundering words here below. For this reason, the advent of the Spirit is invoked, not only on the baptized gathered for the Supper, but also on their gifts, so that the food of which they are about to partake with thanksgiving may not belong to the order of the flesh which serves for nought but that it may be for them—to use the eucharistic terminology which had become traditional, it would seem, in the time of Paul—spiritual food and drink, permeated with the Spirit and consequently with the presence of the Kingdom.[9] The bread and the wine are not to stay "immobilized" at the threshold of the Kingdom, since Christ chose them as symbols which enable us to taste how good the Lord is. We shall return to this theme when we speak of the Supper as living bread.

The importance of the place where the epiklesis occurs must also be stressed: it follows the anamnesis at least in the Syro-Byzantine tradition. What can be concluded from its position? First, that it was the intention to give to the unfolding of the eucharistic liturgy the trinitarian rhythm of the confessions of faith: after celebrating the work of the Father in the preface and after remembering the work of the Son in the anamnesis, the work of the Holy Spirit is invoked in the epiklesis. Neglect of the epiklesis consequently presupposes, implicitly in any case, the whittling down of the affirmation of the Creed in which the Church professes to offer the same adoration and glory to the Spirit as it offers to the Father and the Son. But the position of the epiklesis after the words of institution shows that the recitation of these words is not sufficient in itself to turn the Supper into a true eschatalogical event. It is at this point that the epiklesis seems to offer a real protection to the anamnesis against the danger of magic, without in any sense depriving the Supper of its virtue: it challenges the idea that the mere recitation of the words which marked the institution of the Supper constitutes the Supper without there being any need to beseech the Holy Spirit Himself to complete what is then taking place.

It is at this point that the debate must be lifted above susceptibilities and passions, that the West must be willing to listen patiently to the Orthodox Church, without immediately retorting that the eucharistic practice of the Orthodox as often appears to infringe the liberty of God as does the Roman practice of the Mass. Perhaps on this issue Protestants might be able to bring closer understanding by a fraternal interrogation of both sides. Indeed it is not erroneous to attribute to the attenuation and eventual disappearance of an explicit epiklesis after the words of institution in the western catholic tradition, some of the strongest reasons for the opposition of the Reformers to the Roman Mass: the increasing tendency for the Mass to have an exclusively sacrificial orientation[10]—with votive and paid masses, the concentration of the consecrating power solely in the words of institution—with the eucharistic devotion peculiar to the Roman tradition (Corpus Christi, reservation, and adoration of the Blessed Sacrament), with over-emphasis on the clergy in relation to the laity (the priest having the power and the right to effect the real presence of the Son in the bread and wine; the privilege of communicating in both kinds; the power of excommunicating, even temporarily, baptized children), etc.

The question will be raised why the Reformers, who criticized the Roman Mass for what most distinguished it from the liturgical doctrine of the East, did not simply correct this by restoring, on theological grounds, an epiklesis after the anamnesis? One hesitates to attribute this failure to a lack of liturgical erudition, since sporadic attempts were made to reintroduce an epiklesis—but before the words of institution. If the epiklesis was not restored, it was because the Reformers were in basic agreement with the Western tradition which had fixed the moment of the consecration at the point where the words of institution were recited, as against St. Cyril of Jerusalem who fixed it at the moment of the epiklesis. When you read the confessional writings of the Reformers it is clear that they shared the Augustinian principle: *accedit verbum ad elementum et fit sacramentum.* The later Helvetic Confession is very definite on this point, "That which beforehand was not Sacrament is made a Sacrament by the word of God; more especially as it is consecrated by the Word and declared to be sanctified by Him who ordained it."[11]

One may wonder, then, if the failure of the Reformers to purify the eucharistic life of the West does not arise from the fact that, by taking their stand on the ground of eastern pneumatology, they had no access to a *tertium* which would have enabled them to remove the Roman abuses and distortions without at the same time dislodging the Supper from its central place in the life of the Church. Now the pneumatology of the West, at least in the way Western theologians have generally understood the addition of *filioque* to the Nicene Creed, does not seem to have been able to avoid the dilemma between an institutional, clerical and "filioquist" ecclesiology which impinges on God's freedom and an "illuminist" absence of ecclesiology which threatens its own orthodoxy because it makes the Holy Spirit a competitive rival of the Son. Certainly that is not the last word; but I think that the Orthodox insistence on recognizing in the position of the epiklesis after the anamnesis a vital crux for theological reflection must be taken very seriously by Roman Catholics and Protestants.

In the tradition which has retained it, the epiklesis is pronounced, as is the anamnesis, in the first person plural. It is the people who, through the lips of the minister, invoke the Spirit. This, too, is important because the clergy-people balance is not threatened as it is when the culminating moment of the eucharistic action is fixed at the moment of the pronouncement of the words of institution. Indeed, in that case, the one who pronounces them acquires a power over the redemptive event which undoubtedly threatens the ministerial nature of his authority. And even if one tries to remove this threat by insisting on the fact that the eucharistic event becomes *ex opere operato*, by the very fact of its being effected in this way rather than *ex opere operantis*, by the fact of its being performed by some man, it still remains, as is abundantly proved by the arguments brought by the Reformers against the abuses of authority by the Roman clergy.

Here again, the last word has not been spoken, and a rediscovery of the epiklesis in the first person plural will not magically reinstate in their reciprocal rights and duties the ministers of Christ and the people of God among whom they are to exercise their ministry. I believe, however, that this right to pray all together for the life-giving Spirit to come "on *us* and on our gifts", if it is truly respected, cannot fail to bring an immediate and deeper awareness of the royal priesthood of the people of God, of their eschatalogical reality and of the proper status of a ministry which is neither blown up by its theurgic power nor deflated by over-protestation against this exaggeration. This joint epiklesis, because it is pronounced "on us and on our gifts", also protects the Eucharist against a reduction of the sacrificial significance of the Supper to the anamnesis of the expiatory death of Christ so as to set the Church and what she has brought in obedience to the orders of Christ within the action of the offering. Once again a false dilemma may be avoided: the choice between a repetition of the sacrifice (which closely threatens its uniqueness and sufficiency) and a conception of the Supper robbed of all its sacrificial power, as if there could be no alternative to what must rightly be opposed (with the result that you are aloof from any oblative movement, isolated from the unanimous ancient tradition, and uncertain of the deep and true reasons for celebrating the Supper).

NOTES

[1] Quoted by F. J. Leenhardt, *Le sacrement de la sainte cène*, Neuchâtel and Paris, 1948, p. 18; cf. *ibid.*, p. 55.

[2] *Essays on the Lord's Supper*, 1958, pp. 64–70.

[3] Anamnesis of the Liturgy of St. John Chrysostom.

[4] The ministry of the Word is, of course, exercised at other times than when the Church meets for the Eucharist.

[5] The hypothesis of J. Jeremias, *op. cit.*, pp. 101 f.

[6] *Ibid.*, pp. 229–46.

[7] Benoit says this of *Abendmahlsworte Jesu*, 2nd edition, Göttingen, 1949 in his 'Le récit de la cène dans Luc XXII, 15–20', *Revue Biblique*, 1939, p. 242.

[8] It is the object of the prayer of Jesus to His Father (John 14: 16) and the object of the prayers of the Church (cf. Luke 11: 13 and the variant ἐλθέτω τό ἅγιον πνεῦμά σου καὶ καταρίσατω ἡμᾶς in Luke's version of the Lord's Prayer; cf. also Acts 4: 24–31, probably also Acts 1: 14). This prayer for the gift of the

Spirit is especially linked with baptisms (Acts 8: 15) and ordinations (Acts 6: 6
13: 3; 14:23).

[9] E. Käsemann rightly thinks that when Paul spoke of πνευμάτικὸν βρῶμα and
πνευματικὸν πόμα (1 Cor. 10: 31) he was making use of eucharistic terminology
already in existence in early Christian catecheses.

[10] Quite bluntly Y. Brilioth observes "In any case it is clear that the Epiklesi
has been ousted by the thought of the sacrifice" (op. cit., p. 77).

[11] "Nam verbo Dei fiunt, quae antea non fuerunt, sacramenta . . . Con-
secrantur enim verbo, et sanctificata esse ostenduntur ab eo qui instituit". (W
Niesel, Bekennenschriften und Kirchenordnungen der nach Gottes Wort reformierten
Kirche, München, s.d., p. 260.)

II

THE EUCHARIST, REVELATION OF THE LIMITATIONS
AND OF THE PLENITUDE OF THE CHURCH

'BECAUSE THERE IS one loaf, we who are many are one body, for we all partake of the same loaf." (1 Cor. 10: 17). This Pauline claim, which only makes sense if this unique bread is the Body of Christ, means that the Supper constitutes the Church and reveals her.

The Church first appears, historically and sociologically, as a local congregation, and it is only as the Church shows proofs, in depth, of his localization that she is seen as the catholic community. To realize how the Supper reveals the limitations of the Church in no sense calls into question her plenitude.

When one says that the Supper reveals the limitations of the Church, one is stating that the Supper makes manifest the baptismal, apostolic and local character of the Church. These three adjectives must be studied more closely.

Entry to the Church comes after death to self. That is the meaning of the baptismal nature of the Church: she is a centre of resurrection, renewal and of future existence, since she gathers together the men and women who have confessed that their *raison d'être*, the profoundest truth about themselves, is found, not in themselves, but in the Jew, Jesus of Nazareth, who is acknowledged and glorified as Messiah of Israel and Saviour of the world. This is why the Church of necessity adopts an authoritative line over her adherents, proclaiming herself as a community with its own rules, requirements and discipline. The Supper shows forth this baptismal community by enabling it to be constantly recreated and to be aware of its true nature.

There is then an intimate link between the Supper and Baptism: it is the meal eaten by the baptized, it restores and confirms those who communicate and enables them to grow into their baptismal resurrection, it reveals the Church as a community of those who know what succeeds the world and its history and who already live by it. The

37

Church is not of the world. From which fact arises the necessity for an ecclesiastical discipline.

On this subject two matters are to be noted. It is idle to desire a eucharistic discipline if one has abandoned baptismal discipline, for the former presupposes and confirms the latter: a eucharistic discipline which does not translate the baptismal discipline into effective action would be artificial, suspect and altogether detestable. If obedience to the Gospel demands a rediscovery of discipline, it is this baptismal discipline which must first be rediscovered, otherwise the eucharistic discipline will be without foundation. When one sees the situation of the Church in the present-day world, one may well ask if one of the most urgent tasks which faces all the Churches does not consist in joining forces in order to subject baptismal practice to a criticism as radical and severe as was the criticism to which the Reformation subjected the eucharistic practice of the medieval West. So much for the first observation.

The second concerns the eucharistic discipline of the "younger" Churches. Today they are seeking to shake it off because the "older" Churches have allowed it to degenerate or have neglected it, and they fail to see why they should be expected to maintain it simply because they are "younger" (or perhaps even more because the majority of their members are non-whites). To keep their Church under a discipline which the white West no longer practises is to impede the emancipation of their Church and its progress towards adulthood. That they do not desire this is easily understood. It is well-known, too, that discipline is often exerted in a way which is at variance with the Gospel, doubtless because the eucharistic life, the only normal standard of a post-baptismal discipline, does not play, at least in the Protestant mission fields, the part which it is called to play in the Christian Church.

But discipline is not a pedagogic expedient which would lead, in the history of this world, to a moment when it would cease to be necessary because one would have allegedly emerged from childhood. It is only in the Kingdom of God that discipline will cease to exist, because therein it will no longer be necessary. To dispense with it before that is to imagine that the Kingdom is already established in history or else to refuse to acknowledge any ontological link between the Church and the Kingdom.

It would be very desirable that the "younger" Churches, instead of imitating our practices, should take us sternly to task and ask us who has given us the right to opt out of the eschatological situation (where there are ambiguity, disputes and strife and for which a discipline is therefore necessary), in which Christ, between His Ascension and His Parousia, keeps His Church alive.

While revealing the limitations of the Church, the Supper in the second place reveals her apostolic nature. For if the Church is set apart from the world, it is not that she alone is to be sheltered from the shocks of history and the wrath of God, it is that she may enter the world to be salt and light therein. My last chapter will take up this problem in greater detail; I shall, therefore, only pause for the following brief remark which touches on one of the numerous aspects of the relation between the Word and the sacrament.

It is impossible to limit the Word. The Word leads the way and will not tolerate anything which would prevent it from gaining ground. It seeks to reach out to everything because the love of God, the Gospel, prevails over His anger and loathing. The Word is clearly seen as the bearer of the "prevenient grace" of God, to have recourse to a scholastic term. It is the aim of the Word to penetrate everything, to reconcile everything, to seep into the narrowest crevices, and any resistance it meets arises from the sin of men; what happened on Good Friday is there to prove it. I believe that it is impossible to attribute any such function to the sacrament. Seen from this angle—not the only angle, I admit—its function is rather to mark not how far the Word has gone, but how far it has been received, what it may seal and bring within the Divine Covenant.[1] Far from giving the Church a chance of opting out of her divine mission, the sacrament on the contrary simplifies and purifies the missionary obligation by delineating the frontier between the Church and the world: it shows her what is the essential point from which she may carry the Gospel to the world, and to which she must retire to give thanks and to intercede.

The Supper, in revealing the limitations of the Church, reveals its *local* character. Even if those whom the Supper nourishes have become strangers to the world through their baptism, even if the place where they foregather is for them only a sojourning place, a stage on their exodus, it is nevertheless still there, in their own homes, that they must be and act as the Church of God. Whence the essential importance of the local Church, the epiphany *hic et nunc* of the Holy Church of God. Indeed, if passing through the waters of baptism brings death, it also brings resurrection, and he whom it raises to life is the same person as he whom it brought to death: baptism does not do away with personal identity, rather it purifies and enhances it. So the Church, precisely at the central moment of her life, namely the Supper, has the clear duty of being the Church in such-and-such a place and at such-and-such a time. Indeed, although liberated from her environment so as to be in a position to confront it, the Church is also, secretly, the pledge of the future, the earnest or the first-fruits of the place and the age in which she is planted. She bears its future as Noah and his ark bore the future of that which was about to be swallowed up by the flood.

The local Church is guarantor and guardian "of the glory and the honour" of the place where she is (cf. Rev. 21: 26), of the hope of the future of such-and-such a spot, of such-and-such a moment in the world and its history. This is why we must never confuse unity in the Church with uniformity of Churches. A general levelling of Churches, their alignment to one single type of local Church, of which all the others under threat of sanctions would be an identical replica, would prejudice one of the really basic missions of the Church: that of welcoming to her Eucharist, through the narrow road of the baptismal process, those elements which make up the cultural and spiritual individuality of the time-place setting in which the Church finds herself. From this springs the right of a local Church to be "national", the people of God as it is gathered, not out of humanity looked upon as a general anthropological concept, but out of such-and-such a nation (in the N.T. sense of this term).[2]

If this is given due weight, the problem which then arises is how far a Church can encourage "nationality" without ceasing to be a Church, what is the norm which enables her to attest at one and the same time that she is indeed the Church which loves Jesus Christ, but that it is Jesus Christ that she loves. From the beginning and until the Parousia the Church has experienced, and doubtless will continue to experience, strong tensions on this point. But it must be remembered also that the more aware a Church is of her eschatological nature, the more she seeks primarily the Kingdom, the less she settles down in the world, the stronger in her is the sense of "inter- and trans-national" solidarity of the Church. For this reason the New Testament on the whole lays more stress on unity in the Church than on diversity of Churches.

By way of example of the limitations and of the play of the local individuality of Churches in the one Church, the question of the eucharistic species may be taken. It is a delicate question and at this stage I do not want to do more than call attention to it.

We are familiar with the species chosen by Christ at the time of the Institution: from what constituted the Jewish paschal meal (or possibly another type of Jewish communal religious meal), Jesus chose, He took (ἔλαβεν, λαβών) bread and a cup of wine. The bread must have been unleavened; the wine must have been red, apparently diluted with a little water. In the primitive Church these elements were respected,[3] with this difference that the bread was ordinary bread, leavened, since the Jewish Passover had now been fulfilled and since the Eucharist was celebrated at least every Sunday. By the sixteenth century the Roman West had fairly generally abandoned red wine in favour of white; the custom had also arisen, between the ninth and the eleventh centuries, of replacing the leavened bread with wafers of unleavened bread. But no other eucharistic species are known, even in countries where wheat is not grown and in particular where the vine could not be acclimatized. The Reformers were hesitant. On the whole Anglicans and Lutherans clung to what had become usual in the West, while the Reformed (Calvinists) reverted to the ancient usage, the *panis cibarius*, ordinary bread. As a general rule, the Reformers renounced the practice of adding water to the wine, although this did not indicate any solidarity with the Armenians who objected to water being added to the wine (or yeast to the bread) because they were Monophysites.[4] Bread and wine remain the normal elements of the Churches which are members of the World Council, as also of the Roman Church.

Is this remarkable traditional unanimity characteristic of the Supper? Could one not celebrate it with other elements, provided that one element is to be eaten and the other drunk, provided—as the Dutch Reformed theologian Hermannus Witsius (1636–1708) suggested— that food and drink are involved "which can serve the purpose of bread and wine and which have the ability to strengthen the body and gladden the heart?"

At first sight, there are two possible answers, each backed by valid reasons. If one regards the Supper as a meal prepared by such-and-such a local Church and where Christ is the invited guest (in the sense of Luke 24: 29 ff.; Rev. 3: 20) then one fails to understand why this meal must consist of the bread and wine which are basic foods in the Mediterranean area. The universality of His lordship ought on the contrary to enable Christ to sanctify rice or tapioca just as well as bread, and beer or palm-wine just as well as grape wine, and to use these to prefigure the Messianic feast. On the other hand, if it is Christ who sets up His table in such-and-such a local Church, He it is who will choose the elements.

It is the second alternative which tradition has retained and, I think, for very good reasons, of which I emphasize three. This solution seems to be right, first of all, because the initiative in providing the Supper springs not from the Church but from Christ. The Church has only to obey an order from Christ.

Then, this solution seems right because the Supper loses its power if it is reduced to a meal where Christ is invited in the hope that thereby it will become a Messianic meal. If it were only that, I see no strong reason for not allowing elements other than bread and wine. But if it is such a meal, that is not its sole nature: it is anamnesis and participation in the body and blood of Christ which assume most definitely the presence of the elements which Jesus used when He instituted the Supper and with which He claimed to be identified.

Finally, I wonder whether Christ's choice of bread and wine as eucharistic elements should not be understood in the light of the fact that when Jesus became man, He became a Jew, and therefore there are definite Christological reasons for respecting the traditional elements. It was in Jesus of Nazareth that the eternal Son of God came to encounter and to save *all* men. By becoming involved in "Jewishness", by assuming this scandalous limitation, He appeals also to men to become involved in this "Jewishness", to accept the fact that they can neither recognize nor encounter Him except in this distant past and in this particular nation to which He belonged. This "Jewishness" of Christ seems to me as irrevocable as the election of Israel (cf. Rom. 11: 29), and equally scandalous, and to wish to reject it threatens to separate Christ from His incarnation and turn Him into a vague spiritual principle. Because in a certain sense you cannot avoid becoming a Jew when you become a Christian, it seems to me that these elements of the Jewish paschal meal (or of other Jewish religious meals), the bread and the wine, must be honoured. It is in no sense a question of judaizing after the manner of those who wished to impose circumcision on those pagans who became believers. Judaizing is a soteriological anachronism; it calls into question the decisive, radically renewing nature of Christ's advent. To remember that this advent must be respected in its uniqueness and particularity (of race, place, date) is not judaizing, it is preaching the Gospel.

However, the problem of the "eucharistic menu" arises especially in mission areas where bread and wine are unfamiliar. What is one to do in this situation? I suggest the three following rules.

(1) It must be demonstrated, by quoting the numerous historical examples, that whenever the Church has experienced a great missionary advance, she has found herself faced by the problem of celebrating the Eucharist in places where the traditional eucharistic elements are unknown. Nearly always she has held to the traditional elements, even in countries where, for example, the vine, if transplanted, could never become acclimatized, and where consequently the eucharistic elements have to be imported. Such an explanation could have the marginal, but welcome, result of showing to the Christian communities of Asia, Africa and of the Northern hemisphere, that even to Europeans the Gospel was once foreign.

(2) One must agree to a fraternal discussion of the question without taking any local decision except in agreement with the other Churches. In this matter, traditional unanimity is too firmly anchored for us hastily to assign the choice of the eucharistic species to the category of *non necessaria* in which the law of liberty is operative. It may be that this debate will show that the Supper loses neither its meaning nor its efficacy if it is celebrated with elements other than those chosen by Jesus. At a first estimate I do not accept this, but it would be hasty to come to this conclusion out of hand. This possibility should be left open, but open not to some arbitrary and "separatist" act by some local Church which would set itself, on its own authority, against the Gospel records and unanimous tradition, but open to mutual and brotherly reflection. For even if doctrinally such an individual and unilateral action can hardly be thought of as heresy, it would in any case be schismatic and arrogant.

(3) One must seriously wonder whether the occasional revival of the Agape would not correspond in a valid way to the "localization" of such-and-such a Church gathered for the Eucharist, in the sense that the elements of this Agape (although out of line with the traditional eucharistic elements yet still serving their purpose) would enable such a local Church to avow her "national" limitations without compromising her catholic position. I believe that, by looking in this direction, one could intelligently help the "younger" Churches who often rebel against having to celebrate the Supper "in the European manner" (often forgetting that with all the Churches, including those of Europe, they are celebrating it "in the Jewish manner").

This, however, would not prevent, in exceptional circumstances, the Supper from being celebrated with other elements than bread and wine.

By setting up the Church, the Supper does more than reveal her limitations, it reveals also her plenitude. This is found only within the limitations emphasized, as it is in Jesus of Nazareth that God caused the fullness of His divinity to dwell. It is in the local Church then that the fullness of the Church must be sought. The Eucharist which gathers this local Church reveals the plenitude of the Church by revealing her structure and her mystery.

First, the Supper is the moment at which the structure of the Church becomes apparent, by the very fact that the Supper brings the Church into view and makes her visible by gathering her members together.

Negatively, this means that the elements of ecclesiastical structure and organization which normally have no eucharistic function or reference are unrelated to the essential nature of the Church and therefore irrelevant for ecclesiology, if not suspect. It is indeed possible to state that the celebration of the Supper, the heart and centre of the Christian community, provides the key to the interpretation of the structures of the Church, and consequently prevents any confusion between the institutions which are essential to the Church and her juridical organization. This organization is necessary to the institutions, but the two do not necessarily coincide, even though the function of the juridical organization is to express, and to express to the fullest possible extent, the structure which is essential to the Church. This eucharistic reference will thus enable us to combat that voracious bureaucracy which menaces every social body, by seeking to maintain the organization of the Church in simplicity and coherence.

Positively, this means that because of the Supper, for it and through it, the Church appears as an ordered body. Reduced to its basic expression, the structure of the Church which the Supper reveals comprises, in the unity of shared salvation, two poles: a shepherd and a flock, a father and a family, a visitor and those he visits, a witness of Christ and members of His body. This polarity affirms a necessary reciprocal relationship, the impossibility for the one to exist without the other. Without a flock a shepherd ceases to be a shepherd, but without a shepherd the sheep are not a flock; without a family a father ceases to be a father, but without a father the children are orphans; without people to visit a man in whom and by whom God visits His people, that is to say an ἐπίσκοπος loses his *raison d'être* and becomes a parasite, but without this visitor the others would be waifs and strays.

I have used these three Biblical images deliberately because they show that the first are given to the second and the latter entrusted to the former, that they are necessary to each other, called to love each other without becoming identical. This polarity carries absolutely no implication that either pole is to be disqualified in favour of the other; it entails no privilege in the matter of salvation; it could never be an occasion for scorn from one side, of rebellious demand from the other; and especially, since it is no longer a matter of the structure of the Church but of salvation, it restores to the people those who are commanded to feed them in Christ's name, so that it may be quite clear that Christ is the arch-shepherd, and that if they represent Him, they do not replace Him (1 Pet. 5: 4). On the level of the structure of the Church this polarity, however, teaches God's people that He has not abandoned them and that Christ, between His ascension and His second coming, desires to comfort them by giving them His ministers to be shepherds, fathers and bishops.

It is admitted that there is a coincidence between the institution of the Supper and the foundation of the Church (in the sociological sense). We must go into detail: the institution of the Supper is not only the moment of the institution of the Church, but also that of the institution of the ministry for and in the Church. It is in this sense that doubtless we are to interpret the fact that at the Last Supper Jesus had only the Twelve with Him—those who were to teach the Church to celebrate the Supper.[5] It is perhaps to this time that one must allocate the primary rôle which St. Peter plays in the apostolic collegium if it is true (as O. Cullmann has shown it to be probable) that Matthew 16: 17 ff. must be interpreted through theological parallelism, even chronological parallelism, with Luke 22: 31.

We shall, in the next chapter, resume the discussion of the body of the faithful as an essential element in the structure of the Church. To avoid too much repetition, we shall here concentrate on the ministry as revealed by the Supper, after underlining that the Supper reveals the fundamental structure of the Church (shepherd—flock) on condition that the flock obtains its pasture, that it does not become a mere spectator of a liturgical performance enacted only by a minister, on condition that the people participate in the Supper by communicating. A eucharistic celebration without the people communicating not only contradicts one of the essential reasons for the institution of the Supper, it warps the very structure of the Church.

But is it possible to say anything which is historically precise and accurate concerning the ministry responsible for the Eucharist? A definite position was taken up from the time of Ignatius of Antioch and throughout the whole course of the Church's tradition, including the Protestant tradition. (It is indeed only recently that certain misgivings have been felt in certain Protestant Churches on this subject.) What tradition asserts is, briefly, that to preside at the Eucharist of such-and-such a Church, one must be authorized by Christ, be acknowledged by the congregation as Christ's envoy, and be recognized by the other local Churches as being able and worthy to exercise this charge and authorized so to do.

What does the New Testament say on this point? It says nothing explicitly. This silence may be interpreted in two ways.[6] It may be interpreted as indifference, as lack of interest in the problem, to which the answer will be given that numerous texts may be found which bear witness to meticulous supervision of the authorization to the public ministry of the Word[7] and that one must postulate parallel supervision over authorization to the ministry of the sacraments, since it was *to the apostles* that the command to celebrate them was given. Or it may be said that it is not explicitly stated because it was taken for granted that the one who presided over the eucharistic assembly should be properly appointed.[8] In my opinion the second alternative should be accepted, for the insistence of later tradition on the link between eucharistic adequacy and the authorization of the one who presides over it seems more an expression of respect for the earliest tradition than an apologia for an innovation.

It is the duty of the head of the family to preside at the meal and it was in this capacity that Jesus instituted the Supper: the one who presides over the Church's Eucharist must then fulfil the same "paternal" function and be recognized as worthy and able to exercise it. This basic structure of shepherd—flock, father—family, bishop—those whom he visits, a structure which demands, moreover, a single shepherd for one flock, can be extended and amplified when the need arises. But such amplifications are only justified if they help to support the fundamental structure rather than hide it. Shepherds will then only be multiplied if the flock is subdivided into several flocks. If the single flock is maintained, it is through auxiliaries that the work of the shepherd will be eased, or by spokesmen of the flock along with the shepherd: this enables us to suggest that the diaconate (assistants to the shepherd) and the presbyterate (collegiate representation of the congregation to advise the pastor and in return to represent him when the need arises)

46

do not introduce into the structure of the Church any elements which are in opposition to her eucharistic nature.[9]

The celebration of the Supper is not only related to the structure of the Church; it enables the mystery of the Church to become apparent. This is a two-fold mystery since the Church is at one and the same time a sign of the presence of the Kingdom of God in the world and a sign of the presence of the world before God. Let us take up these two points briefly.

A eucharistic congregation is a visible token of the real presence of the Kingdom and a foretaste of the Messianic feast. The eschatological character of the eucharistic assembly is so fundamental that we shall return to it in our succeeding chapters. At this point I stress three aspects only. The first is that at the moment when the Church meets in eucharistic worship, the total Christ, head and body (*Christus totus, caput et corpus*, to use the Augustinian formula) is present: the Christ who came, who reigns and who is coming, and in Him, because of Him, with Him, the whole communion of saints, in whom the history of salvation is accomplished. There is no more triumphant challenge to fragmentation, to neglect, to dispersal, to the sectaries, to everything which is (etymologically and spiritually) diabolical than the character (etymologically and spiritually) of the Supper. When it is celebrated, because Jesus Christ is present, all His Church is present with Him, since one cannot have Christ apart from His Church, since it is His will ever to be joined with her. The prefaces, the great eucharistic prayer, the *memento* are the ordinary liturgical expression of this truth.

The second aspect is that each local Church when assembled for eucharistic worship and constituted as a Church by the Eucharist is, by the same title, the same sacrament of the same Kingdom because she celebrates the same Eucharist. In other words, the celebration of the Supper fully establishes the congregation which celebrates as a Church; it identifies the congregation as a messianic people celebrating the history of salvation and therefore integrated into this history by its very eucharistic celebration. The holy Church of God, the spotless Bride of Christ thus finds, in this history, its sacramental attestation where two or three are gathered together in His name to obey His order to break bread and to share the cup of thanksgiving—and so also where the Word of God is proclaimed and discipline exercised, since there is no faithful celebration of the Supper without the proclamation

47

of the Gospel and without respect for the complete otherness of the Church in relation to the powers of this world.

It follows—this is the last aspect which I stress—that it is because the eucharistic gathering is a sacrament of the Kingdom that there lies at one and the same time the possibility and the necessity of a structure which manifests the essential identity and unity among themselves of the local eucharistic gatherings. The possibility of this stems from the understanding of the vital significance of the recognition by one eucharistic congregation of the standing of another as a Church.

Theologically, there is no question of one local Church setting herself up as a canonical Church and using this position to grant to any other local congregation seeking for recognition a certificate of ecclesiality. It is much more an act of grace which is shared because one local Church recognizes herself in another local Church and rejoices to acknowledge, in this other Church, the grace by which she herself lives and which characterizes her life.[10] This is the source of the joy of the pastor of a local Church when he recognizes himself in some way in the pastor of another local Church, because he acknowledges in him the mandate, the authority and the mission which he has also received. This is the source of the joy of the laity of a local Church when they recognize themselves in some way in those of another local Church because they acknowledge in them the faith, the new baptismal life, the hope, the discipline of love by which they themselves live.

This acts reciprocally. The mystery of the Church revealed by this eucharistic identity implies then a mutual recognition of Church by Church, of clergy by clergy, of laity by laity—and this despite the singularities of place and age which enable such-and-such a Church to call herself the Church of God, whether she is in Rome or Geneva, whether she is in the fourth or the twentieth century. Even if one common Eucharist enables each local Church to claim to be the same sacrament of the same Kingdom, if the Eucharist makes possible a basis of unity among the local Churches, it also makes such unity necessary, and this not merely for reasons of solidarity, opportunity and effectiveness, but by reason of these mutual admissions of ecclesiality. This mutual ecclesial recognition would be cancelled out if it were not expressed in a pattern which protects, preserves, checks, and which especially deepens these mutual recognitions in love.[11]

The mystery of the Church is that she is a sign of the presence of the Kingdom of God in each local congregation. But it consists also of her being a sign, in each local congregation, of the presence of the world before the face of God. The Church, one might say, is doubly sacramental, because she stands for the real Presence of the Kingdom of God in and on behalf of this world, and for the real presence of this world before and on behalf of God, but of this world when it has re-discovered its "religious" link as being all-important, of this world when it is willing to admit its true nature as a creation of God, destined to glorify Him in Christ who has saved it. This is why each eucharistic celebration also concerns the world very directly, even if the world ignores or mocks it. It may be stated that the celebration of the Eucharist is one of the Church's most important moments of *political* involvement.

Here it is enough to touch on two aspects of this problem. The first concerns the dimensions of the catholicity of the Church. The eucharistic gathering is "kat'holique" in the full sense of the term, because it represents Christ and the members of Christ gathered from all places and ages, because it embodies all the gifts of grace. But this catholicity is too exuberant, too joyful, too vital, to be confined within these bounds, so that it becomes a promise and an opportunity for the whole world, men and things, even if they do not yet believe in this promise or grasp this opportunity.

All the same, when she celebrates the world's salvation, the Church summons not only believers to the Eucharist; she summons also things of this world: bread, wine, time (for there is a Lord's Day for the Lord's Supper), space (for the Church is visible only when assembled in a particular place). The Apostle Paul speaks of creation sighing as it waits for the manifestation of the Sons of God (Rom. 8: 19). If creation sighs it is because the children of this age idolize her, or despise her, spoil her or shatter her.[12] At the moment of the Eucharist creation finds access again to real worship, recovers her primary orientation which is doxological, and Christians may dare to say that because their worship is something which they received, they did not invent it. Moreover, that is why the Eucharist is the source of culture: in a frag-mentary and clumsy, but, for all that, practical manner, it refashions creation in a symbolized way. A Christian, too, cannot help loving the world; that is, he recognizes therein the Father's good work, and helps it to recover the expression of joy in its beauty and goodness.

Certainly this sharing by the world in the Church's Eucharist must be curbed and controlled. Before it can be externalized it will have to pass through a purification of baptismal form, like those "ministrants", those προσφέροντες that Christians became. But once this step is taken, and regularly recalled, the whole of creation can become an act of worship. Father Tillard, speaking of the catholicity of the eucharistic celebration, said that the Church must be able to purify men and their life "to decant them, in order to transfigure them in the Risen Christ. Not to destroy them but to bring them into the new world of salvation."[13] This is true not only of men; it is true also of the environment in which they live and of the things which constitute this environment. For to be undisputed kings of the world, men must first be its priests—that is the vocation of Christians. Such is the profound reason for their so-called temporal involvement.

The second aspect of the problem here raised is that which makes the Church the world's protectress. She is, as the Epistle of James says, "first-fruits of His creatures" (1: 18). It is then in the shelter of the eucharistic assembly, the fundamental moment of the Church's life, that the world can subsist. Certainly not because the Eucharist possesses an intrinsic apotropaic power: but in the Eucharist there is enacted the anamnesis of the death of Christ which saves and keeps the world.[14] We are here in a sacrificial context which has survived the passage from the Old to the New Covenant without becoming anachronistic. Themes are encountered such as the Royal Priesthood of the People of God (Exod. 19: 6; 1 Pet. 2: 9; Rev. 1: 6; 5: 10) charged, in and through Christ, with a mission to reconcile God and the world, commissioned to proclaim and to translate into living the love of God in the world and to gather up and redirect in her worship the yearnings of creation and satisfy them through her service. One encounters also the theme of the suffering of the Church in and on behalf of the world, as if the Church were the victim which the world, all unawares, offers to God to assure its own life (cf. John 15: 18–16: 4), and it is well known that the union Christ-Church is never more close than in times of persecution.[15] One also encounters the theme of the substitutional character of the Church: simply by her presence she protects the world against its own destruction,[16] for if she occupies the place she is called to occupy, then it is the Church that God sees when He looks at the world, and when He sees her, His love prevails against His wrath.

It is important then to emphasize that the Supper (and indeed the whole eucharistic context) does not isolate the Church from the world but rather reveals her deepest relations with it. If, then, the presence of this world at the time of the Eucharist is only too evident, it is not on the level of the offence that this presence takes effect—the offence of identifying a scrap of bread and a drop of wine with the food and drink of life eternal, the offence of having to identify Christians with a royal priesthood, the offence of having to identify any Sunday morning with the world of the resurrection—it is in a realm where, to see all there is to see, you need other eyes than those with which you were endowed at your first birth.

NOTES

[1] It is for this reason that to bring the concept of prevenient grace into baptism, and particularly into infant baptism, seems to me dangerous, for then the special nature of the sacrament in relation to the Word is no longer respected.

[2] While the diversity which is tolerated in the New Testament does not compromise the *local* unity of the Church, it should not lead to a local confessional pluralism, but only to a "national" pluralism within the Catholic Church.

[3] It is impossible at this point to go into detail about the rare exceptions; they concerned chiefly the cup which was either omitted altogether (communion with bread alone or bread and salt) or filled with water rather than wine. Such customs sprang from Encratite or Gnostic circles and were condemned by the Church (even if here and there communion by bread and water infiltrated for a brief while into the Church).

[4] It is well known that the admixture of water and wine has given place to all sorts of symbolic explanations: the union of Christ and the Church (St. Cyprian), the wounded side of Christ (St. Ambrose), the Two Natures (Eastern tradition—when the addition of *warm* water to the already mixed wine does not symbolize the descent of the Spirit upon the species, the fulfilment of the epiklesis).

[5] J. Jeremias is of the opinion that it is by chance ("das ist sicher Zufall") that nowhere other than in Mark 14: 17 = Matthew 26: 20 (οἱ δώδεκα; cf. Luke 22: 14 οἱ ἀπόστολοι) is it definitely stated that it was with the Twelve that Jesus ate; he even thinks, when it is a question of an eastern text, that this precision does not necessarily imply that the women who had accompanied Jesus were not present (*op. cit.*, pp. 40f.). Nevertheless, this contingency is surprising, as *per contra* it is surprising to find a deliberate mention of the women in passages where an eastern text has no peremptory reasons for so doing.

[6] The hypothesis must not be ruled out that this lack of precision may be due to a deliberate discretion on the part of the New Testament writers concerning anything related to the celebration of the Supper.

[7] Two types of text come to mind: those which warn us against the false prophets and more particularly against the false apostles, and those in which the Apostle Paul defends his apostolic authority against those who questioned it. The fact that he never thinks of defending his right to found churches by having recourse to the duty of witnessing laid upon each believer, but that he vigorously defends the "legal" authorization of his apostleship—as also his collegial unity with the Jerusalem apostles (cf. Gal. 2: 2)—is very indicative. In defending his own apostleship, he is fighting for the full ecclesiastical position of the Churches

which he has founded. Their whole integration into the Body of Christ thus depends, for Paul too, on the authenticity of his apostleship: if he is not truly an apostle, then the Churches which he has gathered are not truly Churches and consequently their members are not assured of being really grafted into the history of salvation.

[8] On this matter it must be noted that the apostles (except perhaps at Jerusalem) do not appear to baptize any other believers than those who, in any town, are the first to be born into the faith, the "first fruits" (1 Cor. 16: 15; cf. Rom. 16: 5). This is why Paul's statement that he had not been sent to baptize (1 Cor. 1: 15 ff.) implies no disregard for baptism. Peter, also, once he is away from Jerusalem, does not appear to have been sent to baptize, for he does not himself baptize Cornelius and his household; he commands that they be baptized (Acts 10: 48) probably by the brethren from Joppa who had accompanied him to Caesarea (Acts 10: 23). Or else he "vets" the baptism administered by someone else (cf. Acts 8: 14 ff.), as Paul too does (cf. Acts 19: 1-7). If one can reckon with the information given by Clement of Rome that the apostles generally appointed as bishops and deacons of the communities which they founded those who were the "first fruits", the first converts in these places, one may suppose that these were the men who, once the local Church had been formed, administered baptism and presided over the Eucharist in that Church (1 Clem. 42: 4).

[9] Very many ecclesiological problems arise at this point. I mention only two. The first concerns the relationship between the theology and the sociology of the Church's structures. It must be stated, were it only on the grounds of the information supplied by the history of the Church, that a single theological structure can be expressed sociologically in different ways. A bishop, for example, can be the sole leader of the people of God in a certain town, but he can also, if there are too many people, delegate part of his functions to one of, or even to all, the members of the presbyteral collegium. Even if the sociology of the episcopal ministry is changed, its theological content remains unaffected. This may suggest that nowadays, instead of trying to invent new ministries to face new tasks, it would be more appropriate boldly to rediscover the sociology of the traditional ministries, reserving the right to invent, as additional ministries, something parallel to what the primitive Church did when she adopted and organized the "minor orders" (which ought not to be institutionalized). The second ecclesiological problem greatly preoccupies the present-day Church, because it is linked with her awareness of her minority position in the world. It is the problem of knowing whether what the sixteenth century Protestants called the discipline of the Church (namely her structure and the specific rules governing her life) had its basis in the Church's worship or in the Church's mission. Everything would be falsified if there were a clear-cut alternative here. I would say (and the matter will be taken up in the final chapter) that the Eucharist precedes the Church's mission in the world *and* follows from it: it is from the Lord's Table that the Church goes out into the world, and it is to this Table that she returns from her mission. In this sense the "eucharistic" pattern in some way dominates the "apostolic" pattern; or, if you prefer it, a eucharistic pattern, which cannot be clearly seen, at the end of the act of worship, as an apostolic pattern is certainly spurious. This indispensable apostolic pattern is not then

parallel to the eucharistic pattern, or superimposed upon it or competitive with it. It is the "weekday" form of the Church's basic "Sunday" pattern. For this reason no choice is to be made, despite the inevitable tensions between the Eucharist and the Apostolate. The Church will be less tempted to make a choice if two conditions are fulfilled: the restitution of the inalienable liturgical rights of the laity and their education in the use of them, and the restitution to the clergy of their inalienable apostolic duties and especially their duty of leading the laity, by example and instruction, into the apostolic task. (A Church whose clergy are so disturbed by the world that they shut themselves up in their churches and parishes is a very sick Church.)

¹⁰ Canonically and juridically it is obvious that this act of grace leading to the recognition of oneself in the other will take the form of negotiations, mutual adjustments with the intention of emphasizing the essential identity, mutual concessions with the intention that lawful differences due to space and time be respected, even eventually of temporary rupture if one of the Churches abandons what enables the other to recognize herself in her (e.g. if she becomes heretical). So long as the Church is in a state of pilgrimage her unity has constantly to be fought for.

¹¹ This essential structure of the unity of the Church in the Churches, under heavy pressure from the earliest times, was lost and has not yet been recovered. To move in the direction of such a recovery (the paramount task of the ecumenical movement), two basic conditions must be fulfilled, although they appear contradictory. The pattern of unity must first of all respect the full ecclesiastical position of local eucharistic assemblies and recognize that they are part of the same sacrament of the same Kingdom. The pattern of unity must then, on the clerical and the lay level, include organs for expressing and carrying out its purposes.

¹² If I think that the Church ought to forbid her members, at the risk of their lives, to take any part in an atomic war, it is because nothing could be more contradictory to the Eucharist than atomic war.

¹³ Cf. J. M. R. Tillard, *L'eucharistie, Pâque de l'Eglise*, Unam sanctam, no. 44, Paris, 1964, p. 164.

¹⁴ "For the bread of God is that which comes down from heaven, and gives life *to the world*" καὶ ζωὴν διδοὺς τῷ κόσμῳ (John 6: 33); "I am the living bread which came down from heaven; if anyone eats of this bread, he will live for ever; and the bread which I shall give for the life *of the world* is my flesh—ἡ σάρξ μού ἐστιν ὑπὲρ τῆς τοῦ κόσμου ζωῆς (John 6: 51).

¹⁵ See Acts 9: 4 f = 22: 7 f = 26: 14 f.; 2 Cor. 1: 5 ff; Phil. 3: 10; Col. 1: 24; 1 Pet. 4: 13.

¹⁶ Texts are as frequent in the Old Testament as in the New Testament: if ten righteous men had been found in Sodom and Gomorrah these cities would have been spared (Gen. 18: 32); the presence of Joseph saves Egypt from famine (Gen. 37–41); as long as David is with him, Saul, although he mistakenly thinks David threatens him, is enabled to live (1 Sam. 18–31); the presence of Paul in the ship guarantees the survival of his fellow-voyagers (Acts 27: 21–38), etc. Conversely, when Lot and his companions left Sodom and Gomorrah, the fire fell on these cities (Gen. 19); when Israel was protected by the blood of a lamb, the angel struck the first-born of the Egyptians (Exod. 12: 29 ff); once Israel had

escaped, the Egyptian army was swallowed up in the Red Sea (Exod. 14–15); it was when David was prevented from protecting him that Saul killed himself (1 Sam. 29–31); it was at that moment when Jesus left the Temple never to return that He announced the fall of Jerusalem (Mark 13 and par.). For this reason I wonder whether the mysterious prophecy of the Church being caught up (1 Thess. 4: 17) does not signify that as long as the Church is in the world the end of the world cannot come about because of the Church's protection. But the world, if it may sometimes guess at this protection, is never certain of it; it is such an improbable favour which is here bestowed on the Church that she has to keep the knowledge of it to herself. There could be no step more false than for the Church to tell the world that she is its guarantor and to say this, for example, so as to cash in on this guarantee in exchange for worldly powers and privileges. In the eyes of the world, the Church has the right to wear only the uniform of a servant or the garb of a victim.

III

COMMUNION WITH CHRIST AND WITH THE BRETHREN

THE SUPPER IS a two-fold communion: it unites Christ and the Church, it unites Christians to one another. These two aspects are indissoluble, the latter being determined and also implied by the former. For clarity of treatment, however, they must be looked at separately; the fact must also be stressed that communion with Christ does not arise as a by-product from communion with the brethren. The truth is rather that communion with Christ assumes and demands that those who, because of their union with Christ, are of one spirit with Him should form one body among themselves.[1] In the Gospel there is far too much emphasis on eschatological power, on the action and presence of another world, for it to be mere humanitarianism, however high-minded, even though of necessity it does have ethical consequences, making its followers eager and able to make the most spontaneous, the boldest experiments in human solidarity and affection.

First of all, the Supper is communion between Christ and the Church. The New Testament presents this in two ways: as communion with Christ and in Christ. This does not appear to be an alternative; rather the two aspects are complementary and this interdependence is found to some extent in all the strata of the New Testament, even though one writer may stress one aspect rather than the other.[2]

The question arises whether it was the fact of sharing food with Christ which gave to the meal the name "Lord's Supper", κυριακὸν δεῖπνον (Cor. 11: 20). At all events, it is clear that this played some considerable part in fixing the liturgical framework of the Supper. It was on the occasion of the last meal of Jesus with His disciples, before His death, that He instituted the Supper, and it must be admitted that if the meals eaten with Jesus played some part in the development of the liturgy and theology of the Eucharist, the latter have also given a certain eucharistic colouring to these meals. One thinks especially of the accounts of the multiplication of the loaves, of the marriage at Cana, above all of the meals eaten with the Risen Lord[3] which play so important a part in the apostolic consciousness of those who describe themselves as "chosen by God as witnesses, who ate and drank with Him (συνεφάγομεν καὶ συνεπίομεν) after He rose from the dead" (Acts 10: 41). The meal which Jesus asks to share as guest with him who opens the door to Him (Rev. 3: 20) also comes to mind.

But the Supper is also communion in Christ: "The cup of blessing which we bless (ὃ εὐλογοῦμεν), is it not a participation in (? of) the blood of Christ (κοινωνία τοῦ αἵματος τοῦ Χριστοῦ)? The bread which we break, is not a participation in (? of) the body of Christ (κοινωνία τοῦ σώματος τοῦ Χριστοῦ)?" (1 Cor. 10: 16). The Supper then is the moment when there comes into being what St. Augustine was to call *Christus totus, caput et corpus.*[4] Paul and John especially emphasize this aspect of communion. Paul does so because for him the intention of the Supper is to incorporate believers into Christ Himself, gift and Giver being received together; John because for him the Supper is the moment when Christ fulfils the promise "he who eats my flesh and drinks my blood abides in me and I in him".[5] On this account it is possible to claim that "through the Eucharist the believer enters into a relationship with Christ as close and as efficacious as that which existed between Jesus and His disciples during His earthly ministry, and even into a closer and more efficacious relationship, seeing that now the redemptive action, the death and resurrection of Christ, has taken place and that the mystery of Christ's Person is revealed to believers and that the Spirit unleashes His power in the Church; in a word, seeing that 'now we no longer know Christ after the flesh', but the glorified Christ united to His Church by His Spirit".[6]

Before going any further, two things must be said. The first is obvious, but it is surprising that it has not been advanced in this context. If the Supper brings Christ and the Church into communion, then they must both be really present, otherwise their communion would be impossible. This is to say, indirectly, that since the New Testament deals so profoundly with the theme of eucharistic communion, this must stem from the apostolic witness that at the Supper the real presence of Christ is as evident as the real presence of the Church which is celebrating the Supper. "To deny that true communion with Jesus Christ is offered to us in the Supper is to make this holy Sacrament inane and ineffective, which is an abominable blasphemy unworthy of being listened to", says John Calvin.[7]

I make the second observation with some hesitation, since the theme to which it is related has fallen so much into disuse: the nuptial theme to illustrate the communion between Christ and the Church. This theme, however, constantly recurs in all the strata of the New Testament. From the time of His incarnation, Jesus is the bridegroom (cf. Mark 2: 20 and par.) and He has His bride (cf. John 3: 29). The coming Kingdom is described as a marriage feast (Matt. 22: 2 ff.; 25: 1 ff.; cf. Luke 12: 36), and Jesus demonstrates the signs that the Kingdom has already come on the occasion of a village wedding (John 2: 1 ff.). St. Paul interprets the rise and history of the Church in terms of an epithalamic typology (2 Cor. 11: 2; Eph. 5: 25 ff.); the Seer announces the consummation of history in terms of the marriage of the Lamb (Rev. 19: 17 ff.), for which the Church makes herself beautiful (Rev. 21: 2) and for which, in that profound harmony with the Spirit which characterizes her life she longs with the cry, *Maranatha*, Come! (Rev. 22: 17, 20).

This figure was regularly used by the Fathers, and, if it has gradually fallen out of use, it is doubtless because, on the one hand, it was difficult to sustain a nuptial similitude with its inevitably indelicate aspects[8] in a Church which had relaxed its conditions of entry,[9] and, on the other hand—and perhaps this is the more cogent reason—because of the abandonment of coherence in the time, and for adults in particular, of the stages in Christian initiation. For it was the first communion which was particularly interpreted in this nuptial perspective: Christian initiation—renunciation of sin, the world and the Devil, confession of the Christian faith, baptism, unction, communion with the returning Christ, all this at the dawn of Easter Day—being a kind of prefiguration *ad personam* of the drama of the end of the world, of the cosmic baptism, of the great purification beyond which it becomes possible at one and the same time to celebrate the wedding feast with the Lord and to become with Him that single Spirit, that $\overset{\text{\'{e}}}{\epsilon}\nu$ $\pi\nu\epsilon\hat{\upsilon}\mu\alpha$ of which the apostle Paul speaks.[10] For this reason the paramount prayer of the Church is "Thy kingdom come" . . . this coming being anticipated as far as is possible in this world on the occasion of the Supper.[11] *Adesto, adesto, Jesu, bone pontifex*, says a Mozarabic prayer,[12] and the Acts of Thomas reports a prayer offered at the time of the catechumens' first communion, in which, on two occasions, the celebrant cries: $\overset{\text{\'{e}}}{\epsilon}\lambda\theta\epsilon$ $\kappa\alpha\grave{\iota}$ $\kappa o\iota\nu\acute{\omega}\nu\eta\sigma o\nu$ $\dot{\eta}\mu\hat{\iota}\nu$ ("Come and enter into communion with us, become one with us, join Thyself to us!")[13]

In the present state of the Church it is doubtless hardly possible to revive this nuptial theme to illustrate the two types of communion between Christ and the Church which the Supper effects. This is to be regretted because this theme facilitates the understanding of the Church's first duty, of the personal nature of the Christian faith and of the situation of the Church in the world. Let us see the implications of this.

What constitutes the joy and pride of the Church is that already she is so closely joined to Christ as to form His body (Eph. 5: 28, 30). What is required primarily of her is that she should love Him who gave Himself for her and remain steadfast in her "first love" (Rev. 2: 4 ff.). She belongs to Christ and exists solely for Him. If she exists also for the world, it is indirectly, because her Lord has vanquished the world and she has been sent to teach Christ to the world by her words and way of life. In order that she may teach Him to the world, the Church is rightly charged with the duty of showing to the world her love for Jesus of Nazareth. The Supper is the place and the moment when the Church is filled with Christ and renews her love.

Emphasis is rightly laid upon the communal nature of the eucharistic life. On the subject of the nuptial theme, it is right too that a warning be given against a mystical union which would read into it the idea of a marriage between Christ and the individual soul. It is surprising to observe, in the Fathers, how easily and quickly the nuptial theme Christ-Church is individualized in the direction of the nuptial theme Christ-individual soul. This is doubtless explained by the fact that the eucharistic catechesis makes its appearance pre-eminently as a catechesis in preparation for the *first* communion which seals and crowns baptism and unction, the personal nature of which cannot be over-emphasized. This is a good thing. For if it is dangerous and false for the believer at the Eucharist to indulge in a private marriage ceremony between Christ and his soul, and in consequence to forget the essentially ecclesial nature of this communion, it is equally false and dangerous if the ecclesial nature (which takes precedence) should attenuate the unique, personal, non-interchangeable nature of the love which Christ and the believer share. It is, therefore, right and proper that there should be a *personal* eucharistic life. This certainly does not imply that the ecclesial significance of the Supper is the result of the adding together of the eucharistic life of individual believers; but in the Church and along with her this communion is mine.

It is also a good thing to show the links between baptism (or martyr-dom) which cannot be other than personal, and communion which is communal without being anonymous. On this point, what St. Luke records of the Pentecost event should be noted: all received the same Spirit, all were baptized with the same fire. However, they were not overwhelmed with a kind of conflagration which turned the whole Church into one single torch; it came upon them in such a way that each of them personally was kindled with a flame which was his own, although it was from the same fire which set his brethren alight (Acts 2: 3).

The nuptial theme applied to the Supper makes it easier to understand the Church's situation in the world. The New Testament speaks of the marriage of Christ and the Church in the present tense. But the intermittency of the eucharistic celebration, the incessant need to say the Lord's Prayer, the fact that the Supper, even if it can hold death back (cf. 1 Cor. 11: 30 ff.) can never abolish it, and, above all, the promises of Jesus concerning His return, are there to remind us that the Eucharist is still no more than a prefiguration of the Marriage of the Lamb (Rev. 19: 7, 9), a foretaste of the wealth of the Promised Land. However, the fragmentary, provisional, debatable nature of the Christ-Church communion celebrated by the Church does not prevent the Church, despite her fumbling attempts to translate her hope into shapes and colours, from making the Eucharist a festival. For this reason a eucharistic liturgy which is not patently beautiful casts a kind of doubt on Christ's presence there.

"Because there is one loaf, we who are many are one body, for we all partake of the same loaf" (1 Cor. 10: 17). The eucharistic Christ-Church communion implies the brotherly eucharistic communion of the members of Christ one with another (cf. 1 Cor. 12: 26; Acts 4: 32; etc.): and this logic is not accidental or marginal, it is so absolutely fundamental that the Christ-Church communion can be challenged when this communion is not expressed in terms of fraternal communion of all those joined to Christ by the Supper. In this sense the Supper is at one and the same time a sacrament of the New Covenant (forging a covenant unity, not only between the Lord and His people, but of very necessity also between all the members of this people) and a sacrament of charity. (In John's Gospel the theme of love constantly recurs in the farewell addresses of Jesus, as if to replace the account of the institution of the Supper which was not recorded at this point in John, for whom the sacrifice on the Cross took its place; 1 John 3: 11–4: 21 demands some kind of eucharistic reference to reach its full significance.) Communion with Christ turns the Church into a body,

His body; for this reason the Church could not exist without the Eucharist; for this reason it is perfectly right that the classical epiklesis invokes the Spirit "upon *us* and upon our gifts" so that both may become the body of Christ.

We must start by emphasizing several characteristic aspects of this fraternal communion through the Eucharist before dwelling on two difficult problems: that of the relationship of the Eucharist with the Agape, and that of intercommunion.

The essential characteristic of this fraternal communion is that it is not of this world. It prefigures the communion, the final gathering of the people of God. Because of this it plays an important part in the ancient liturgical celebration, as is evident in three ways. First, by the prayers for this unity which reveal clearly that it is not within human grasp, that it can only come in answer to prayer. The history of the cult abounds in prayers which beseech God to *congregare in unum*—as the Anaphora of Hippolytus says—the saints who are celebrating the Supper and, in a wider and just as miraculous a way since it overstrides centuries and distances, to gather the Church from the four corners of the earth into the Kingdom as bread is made from corn which has been scattered abroad, and, while waiting for this consummation, to make all the baptized of past, present and future into a community conscious of its destiny, unity and mission.

Paraphrasing the prayer in the Didache, Calvin said: "As the bread which is hallowed for the common use of us all is made from many grains so intermingled that it is impossible to distinguish them one from another, so ought we to be so united among ourselves in an indissoluble friendship, and what is more, we receive there one and the same Body of Christ so as to be made members of it."

The other ancient liturgical attestation of this fraternal communion is the kiss of peace, which precedes the communion. In apostolic practice[14] this kiss shows that those who are about to communicate agree to resume their baptismal status and to renounce everything in this world which is a source of opposition and division, and particularly to be reconciled one to another because they are reconciled to God. They have passed from death to life because they love each other (1 John 3: 14). It was in this way that from the time of the Didache, if not before, the Church understood the order of Christ not to bring one's gift to the altar before asking for forgiveness from the brother one has offended (Matt. 5: 23 f.)

Chiefly this fraternal communion is brought about by the very fact of the faithful participating together in the Supper. The Apostles, the Fathers (and perhaps St. Augustine in particular), the Reformers too (and perhaps Martin Luther in particular), never tire of presenting the Supper as the *vinculum unitatis*, as the primary place for the exercise and expression of unity in the Church. For this reason the faithful who had not been able to join in the celebration were associated in the Supper by the action of the deacons who took to them bread, and perhaps even wine, which had been used in the Eucharist (Justin Martyr, Apol. I, 65: 5; 67: 5). But for that to happen it is essential that the Eucharist should also be a communion! Until the fourth century this was normally the case for all the baptized who were not excommunicated, but from that date the coincidence between Eucharist and communion began to dwindle. This gradual change delivered a grievous blow to the Supper as an event which created the corporate and fraternal unity of the Church.

The reasons for this are numerous. Perhaps they all stem, directly or indirectly, from the weakening of the link between Baptism and the Supper so that reception into baptismal life did not carry with it as a logical and necessary consequence participation in the meal of the baptized, and an ever-widening gap occurred between the circle of the baptized and the circle of the communicants (this being one of the most grievous wounds in the life of the Church). The consequences are well known: a timid shrinking from the wealth of the eucharistic mystery as if it were more "challenging" than the baptismal mystery and a consequent scrupulousness about taking advantage of it; a progressive reduction of this eschatological and sacerdotal character of the whole Church to priests and monks (who become more and more clerical) combined logically with a progressive secularization of the laity; the multiplication of eucharistic services uprooted from the context of congregational participation and a rapid predominance, in eucharistic theology and practice, of the sacrificial element over the elements of communion and eschatology which are just as fundamental to the Supper; the banishing of the celebration into a sanctuary, and its limitation to a language which no longer directly involved the assembled people, etc.

It is only fair, among the fatal consequences of this widening gulf, from the fourth century on, between the circle of the baptized and that of the communicants, to include the way the Reformers tried to restore the eucharistic life: namely the abolition of the earlier unanimous traditional link between Sunday and the eucharistic celebration, and the reduction, for pastoral reasons, of eucharistic celebrations to the number that people (accustomed for three centuries to communicate only once a year) could tolerate. On quite respectable theological grounds it is true that the Reformers did not want any celebration of the Supper unless all the faithful who were not excommunicated received communion.

I think that, to find a solution to this difficult problem, one must have the courage to go back to the point where it arose and seek to restore the balance between the circle of the baptized and the circle of communicants and to deliver the Churches out of a sociological situation where the majority undergo baptism (and eventually take their *first* communion) and only the minority share in the eucharistic life. So long as the Church does not have the courage to do this, so long as baptism is not governed by the same care and the same intention as the Supper, the Churches run the risk of being condemned to one or other of the errors between which they have been oscillating for centuries: either celebrations of the Eucharist without this being consummated by the communion of the baptized people[15] or celebrations of the Lord's Day without celebrating the Lord's Supper.

While dealing with the Supper as the place and time for fraternal communion it is necessary to speak of the Agape. But that is not easy: first, because the available historical information does not lead to firm convictions; secondly, because the Agape offers to the liturgical and pastoral life of the modern Church opportunities which it would be foolish not to take seriously.

From the historical point of view, one must draw a line between information which is certain and information which is subject to various interpretations. What does seem certain to me is that the Agape was not instituted by Christ as a meal imparting eternal life. It is not of the Agape that John 6: 51–58 speaks; it was what remained over, not after the Agape but after a eucharistic meal that, at a very early date, the deacons took to those of the faithful who had not been able to join in the Christian assembly; and the most ancient liturgical texts, which began with the accounts of the institution of the Supper, showed no direct interest in the Agape. It is also certain that the Eucharist was instituted at the time of a meal[16] and that in the earliest times it was celebrated at the end of a communal meal; it may also be taken for granted—at least in the Palestinian churches—that these meals also had a certain liturgical structure and thus a certain religious significance, and consequently had some kinship with such religious meals as the Jews partook of at the time of Jesus. It seems certain, too, that the Agape was not open to all and sundry, but only to members of the Church.[17] Finally, it is certain that the Eucharist soon became separated from these communal meals, and that these meals, when they ceased to be the "social" framework for the celebration of the Eucharist, soon died out.

On the other hand, the information which is not clear relates to three points. The first has no real importance since it is a matter of terminology.[18] The other two concern the interpretation of 1 Corinthians 11 and the theological reasons which led to the separation of the Agape and the Eucharist. Scholars do not agree on the way of interpreting St. Paul's protest about the meals at Corinth. The Apostle argues that the "Lord's meal" is at stake ($\kappa\upsilon\rho\iota\alpha\kappa\grave{o}\nu$ $\delta\epsilon\hat{\iota}\pi\nu\upsilon\nu$ v. 20). They are rather private meals ($\H{\iota}\delta\iota o\nu$ $\delta\epsilon\hat{\iota}\pi\nu\upsilon\nu$, v. 21) harmful to what Christ instituted and to the tradition of the Church (v. 23–25), incapable of proclaiming the Lord's death until He come (so that He may come?) (v. 26), unworthy of the bread and of the cup of the Lord (v. 27), unsuited to "discern the body" (that is to distinguish the eucharistic food from that of a communal meal rather than incapable of enabling the Church to be aware of her own nature and to secure recognition of herself as the Body of Christ) (v. 29), and because of this, these meals carry condemnation and death rather than blessing and life.

The question at issue is to know how St. Paul intended to remedy this situation. He lays down that the meal shall be held *in common* (v. 21), that it shall not be begun until *all* the faithful have been able to come together (v. 33). Then there is this interpolation at v. 22, "Do you not have houses to eat and drink in?" This can have one of two diametrically opposite meanings. Either it is a command to separate the Lord's Supper, celebrated as He celebrated it on the night when He was betrayed, from the communal meals which, by their abuses, distort the Eucharist itself. (The Apostle Paul would then be the originator of the movement which finally detached the Eucharist from its frame, the Agape; this is the opinion of the majority of the expositors: let Christians eat at home!) Or it is a command to restore to the communal meal its full significance, because for other types of meals, for the $\H{\iota}\delta\iota\alpha$ $\delta\epsilon\hat{\iota}\pi\nu\alpha$, there are hostelries. On this interpretation the Apostle was protesting against an over-estimate of the Eucharist which would make the Agape insignificant. The later history of the Church seems to show that the former alternative is to be preferred.

As for the reasons which led to the separation of the Agape from the Eucharist, it is often assumed that it was due to a progressive sacramentalization of the eucharistic event, to a sacerdotalization of the clergy, to a paganization of the Church's faith, that is, to a kind of falling away from the original purity of the Church.

I confess that I find these reasons hardly convincing. Rather I call attention to two things: first, it was not the Agape, the "framework-meal", which constituted what Christ specifically instituted for the life of the Church, but the *new* thing He created during the meal on the night when He was betrayed. (The Agape could then wither away as a chestnut bur withers without involving the nut which it had to protect and allow to ripen.) Then I call attention to three New Testament texts which speak expressly and undeniably of the Agape (1 Cor. 11: 17–34; 2 Pet. 2: 13; Jude 12) and which see in it a source of difficulty for the unity and life of the Church. To these may perhaps be added three more marginal reasons: the difficulty in a pagan-Christian environment of observing Jewish traditions of communal meals, the victory for the sobriety of the apostolic witness in the matter of eschatology over the illuminist tendencies, and the numerical growth of the Church, which made it difficult to maintain the Agape without breaking up the local congregation into a number of smaller ones.[19] The abandonment of the Agape would then have been a normal stage in the growth of the Church, and it is difficult to understand how J. A. Jungmann can describe the separation of the Eucharist from the Agape as "perhaps the greatest change in the whole history of the mass".[20]

This very summary historical inquiry enables us to conclude, first of all, that what was distinctive in the Christian assembly is not the Agape, but the Eucharist; then, that the Agape could decline in favour of a Eucharist which increased in importance without the fidelity of the Church to the orders of Christ being compromised; finally, that it is not possible to play off the Agape against the Supper as if the transition from a "meal" to a "cult" was a sign of apostasy, and as if the alleged non-theological simplicity of the Agape was redolent of the spring-time and innocence of the Church.

Having said this, one must ask whether a rediscovery of the Agape would not be desirable for the Church of today. An emphatic and affimative answer must be given, but on two conditions. The first is that there should be no intention of reviving the setting of the Eucharist during a meal which is hinted at in the ancient texts. What the New

Testament reveals of the Church is normative for the Church in every age and place. But one must differentiate between the content and the form (sociological, cultural, historical) of this revelation. This form can change according to new sociological, cultural or historic situations. But even in this case this New Testament form remains of the utmost importance, for it is an invitation addressed to the Church in other situations to express the *content* of what the Church is as freely as the New Testament form expressed this content. On the other hand, one must give proper consideration to the internal development of this datum by taking it in its final canonical content rather than in its earlier elaboration.[21]

The second condition is that the types of Agape to be re-introduced should not be institutionalized. Indeed, nothing is more prejudicial to the genuine institutions of the Church (the duty of proclaiming the evangelical kerygma, baptism, the Supper, the ministry, social service) than the institutionalization of what is not basic to the Church, for it arouses an impatience which threatens the genuine institutions. At this point one can only make certain suggestions. I shall make three.

The work of the Eucharist in creating fraternal communion will be furthered if the love, the Agape, which it engenders, enables the Church (1) to strengthen her internal coherence by an occasional communal meal, for example, after worship, or, at least during the festival seasons, by the faithful being asked to invite each other to their homes for a meal before or after parish worship; (2) to rejoice in being the Church which she is (I have already spoken of this when I suggested that alongside the bread and wine for the Eucharist, there might be a "local" menu for the Agape); (3) to extend its work by acts of service worthy of Him who impoverished Himself to enrich us—in the sense of the gift, each Sunday, "of what one can put by" (1 Cor. 16: 1 f.).

Here the question arises of knowing whether those "diaconal" works which would spring from the Eucharist are to be directed preferentially to brethren in the faith or whether they will augment the works of service which are not directly motivated by the giving and receiving of the bread of life.[22] When you consider what is said on this score by the New Testament—where you will find neither the remorse of a sated post-Christianity and the impatience of a destitute and despairing pre-Christianity, nor the glib promises of demagogues—it is for the brethren in the faith that the gifts which have been gathered should be ear-marked. But this "exclusivism" could not be defended nowadays when it is agreed that the Churches in rich countries should share their gifts with those in poorer countries so that the latter may the more effectively radiate around them the freedom which Christ offers to men as the most real opportunity of a full life.

Intercommunion raises a problem only for the Churches which are in a state of division. Fundamentally the question is: what ought one to do and what can one do when fraternal communion cannot be expressed at the time of the Eucharist on account of schisms, but when the separated Churches still celebrate the Supper in the conviction, on the one hand, of the reality of their communion with the Lord of the Church, and, on the other hand, of the reality of their fraternal communion within the limits of that confessional Church? It is a singularly difficult question to answer and one cannot here attempt more than to supply food for thought on this matter.

Lack of communion may result from numerous causes: (1) Mutual excommunication (e.g. Rome and the Orthodox Church, Rome and the Protestant Churches, the Orthodox and the non-Chalcedonian Churches) or the heritage of earlier or parallel schisms which have not led to a definite disciplinary decision (the Reformation Churches, for example, have never expressly separated from the Orthodox Churches, and nothing could be further from the truth than to think that, because they are in schism with Rome, they cannot also not be in schism with the Orthodox Churches; the Reformed Churches on the Continent have never separated from the Church of England and the scope of their separation from the Churches which subscribe to the Augsburg Confession is open to debate; the Methodist Church never separated from the Reformed and Lutheran Churches of the Continent; the Old Catholic Church did not separate from the Roman Church, etc.). (2) Differences in interpretation of the eucharistic mystery, the refusal (sometimes reciprocal) to admit the validity of the way such-and-such a Church discerns the Lord's Body in the Supper, which leads to her being regarded as a different Church, even a false Church. (3) Conflict over who should preside over the Supper, this right being (or not being) linked to the authorization of Christ granted, in a manner which can be checked, to such-and-such a man to act lawfully in His Name: this conflict then turns first on the need for this authorization, then if agreed, on the manner of checking it, the criterion of recognition being for example—or not being—the linking of the apostolic succession to the diocesan episcopate as the sociological basis of the ministry. (4) The fact that the evangelization of the world has gone on despite the divisions in the Church and that new Christian communities have grown up within the framework of the different Churches from which the missionaries were sent. Lack of communion then has many historical and doctrinal causes of varying degrees of importance but all must be taken into account.

In all this, what is the importance of the traditions and mores of European Christianity? Will it diminish in view of the dechristianization of Europe? Will it disappear beneath the impatient assault of Churches in the non-aligned countries which are separated by obligations which to them are for the most part remote? Will it lose its importance through the urgent request, which laymen—whose baptismal unity is not questioned but who enjoy no eucharistic unity[23]—are beginning to address to the priests, to study, in a spirit of service transcending concern for their own prestige, the chances for a new appraisal of what constitutes the power to verify the authorization granted by Christ to preside in His name over the Eucharist? Will this emphasis yield before the illogicality of the entirely new sociological situation facing Christians, a situation which unites them during the week for the apostolic ministry and divides them on Sunday for the Eucharist?

Further questions arise. Have we the right, for example, in one Church to refuse access to the Lord's Table to a person who in another Church has access to the same Table, and can we refuse him access without refusing to recognize the other Church as a Church? Or, seen from the other side, have we the right to decline his invitation to the Lord's Table on the grounds that the one who invites us does not ask on the same grounds as the one whose invitation we usually accept? Can we, without hypocrisy, come together in eucharistic communion with Christ without afterwards staying together in this communion? These questions, which could be multiplied, stem regularly from a situation in which the reasons for the divisions in the Church are not presented to the ministers and to the faithful in a convincing way, whether because their full significance can no longer be gauged or because they are no longer really convincing.

The justification of a division in the Church can depend on many factors: valid theological factors, factors of pride and stubbornness, sociological factors. For example, it is not theologically wrong that the division which in a certain sociological situation seems to be indispensable and permanent should lose its pungency and its compulsive power in a different sociological situation. When there is a division in the

Church in a state where Christianity is unopposed, her divided state seems much deeper and more irremediable than the same division in a situation where the two parties of the divided Church have to face a majority of non-Christians or of post-Christians. As time passes and forms the framework of the history of salvation, we are able to see that certain divisions which formerly seemed to offer the clear alternatives of salvation or perdition, of conversion or rejection, no longer possess this quality of radical cleavage, but have moved into the realm of differentiations within a common loyalty to Christ. Confessional discrimination is no longer an aspect of separation of the Church from the world but rather a separation within the Church, perhaps no longer justifiable in a changed situation.[24]

All things considered, one is faced with this problem: is it possible to give a right answer to a distorted question, or must the question be corrected before the answer can be given, or is it possible to correct the question by means of the answer given to it?

If one elects to give a right answer to a distorted question, one lands in a double impasse. Either one refuses to broach the subject because, in sound ecclesiology, it is communion, not intercommunion, which is the important thing. In this case, one does not take into account the fact that many schisms, including perhaps some which historically and sociologically seem to go deepest, are not really justified in dividing the Church of Jesus Christ. Or else one approves of intercommunion as the right solution, but one surely does so for one of the four following reasons which are too limited or which are distorted.

Some will approve of intercommunion because of their belief that the divisions are forever insurmountable, permanent, written for all time, in their present form, into the Christian tradition. Intercommunion then becomes the little that one is in a position to accept as a protest against this calamity. But in that event to communicate together becomes a kind of lie and a sin against hope.

Others will approve of intercommunion because they reckon that the divisions are not serious, that, in short, they are not worth mentioning in the presence of the Lord of the Church. But, in that event, why do they not have the courage, the imagination, the will, to explore the real depth of these allegedly negligible divisions so as to smooth them away before taking communion together?

Others again will approve of intercommunion because they think that the divisions are just a pretext that the clerics, the theologians, men of the preceding generations, the whites, the bourgeois, or some other tiresome people, have used to prolong their hold on the poor flock of Christ condemned over and over again to be fleeced. Intercommunion then becomes a claim for liberty against a medley of traditionalist, outmoded, burdensome and hateful ideas. Good. But when it comes to turning this intercommunion into an event detached from the past and the future, when it comes to integrating it into the life of the Church, whose dimensions are by no means all revealed in a brilliant but brief prophetic gesture, when it comes to considering, at the level of liturgy, doctrine and organization, what is being done, one cannot help wondering whether the generous and sweeping impatience which has led to intercommunion would not be productive of far more joy and truth if it were used to lead simply to communion. So when will the laity, the young people, or the members of Churches in the southern hemisphere have the idea of addressing to the clergy, and to their expert advisers, the theologians, a request to negotiate unity within a fixed time,[25] and of doing this, not in a spirit of bravado and pride, but with all respect?[26]

Finally, there are those who will approve of intercommunion because they are of the opinion that the divisions are historico-psychological epiphenomena without any true significance for authentic unity since unity, it is claimed, cannot be external and visible but is internal and invisible. But of what possible value then could this demonstration of *external* unity be, namely intercommunion?

Is there any way out of this impasse without at the same time getting into difficulties by giving the right answer since it does not take into account the real core of the matter (the right answer being that the only valid solution to the problem of intercommunion is communion),[27] or being satisfied with a partial or distorted answer since it attributes to the datum a quasi-canonical authority? Is there any way of proceeding towards the right answer without entirely refusing to give some answer before being able to give a complete and unqualified answer?

I should like at this point to seek for the answer in four directions, starting from the conviction that, if the Eucharist is the seal of unity which has been realized, it is also a factor in the unity which is to be realized.

First of all, those who clamour and those who sigh for intercommunion on the ecumenical level must claim with equal vigour communion in their own Church. There is indeed something suspect in the demand for intercommunion if it is voiced mainly by confessions which have allowed the eucharistic life to dwindle, if not to wither altogether. For if it is those denominations who complain most vigorously about the impossibility of intercommunion, their complaints would lead you to believe that the Supper is too marginal an affair for the admission to it and the organization of it to be surrounded with such meticulous care. Anyone who does not demand more frequent and more faithful communion in his own Church ought to refrain from demanding intercommunion.

Secondly, it ought to be possible for Christians to make a more generous use of what is called "limited open communion" or "communion by mutual dispensation". For example, when a member of the Swiss Reformed Church is in England or in Sweden, his ecclesiastical conscience is likely to be influenced more by his solidarity with anti-Roman protestantism of the sixteenth century than by loyalty to his own denomination. His Church will then be in England the non-Roman Church of the land, namely the Anglican Church, and in Sweden the Lutheran Church, because in Switzerland his Church which corresponds to his *sentire ecclesiam* is not so much the Reformed Church with its own particular denominational emphasis, but the non-Roman Church which in this case happens to be the Reformed Church. He ought then to be able to communicate without difficulty in the Anglican Church in England and in the Lutheran Church in Sweden. And conversely. If this same Swiss protestant finds himself in a country where there is a marked denominational pluralism, he ought to be able to make a choice which he has no opportunity of doing at home, and so not to be taken for a Presbyterian in the United States, for example, because in his own country, if he does not want to be either a Roman Catholic or a sectarian, he cannot in effect be anything else but a member of the Reformed Church. One may even wonder if for a time of enforced denominational "exile", this arrangement for a eucharistic dispensation ought not to be adopted, without there being any denominational desertion involved but just in the name of Christian hospitality, by all the Churches which recognize the validity of the stranger's baptism.[28]

A third problem is raised by the possibility or otherwise of experiments of temporary intercommunion, for example at the time of ecumenical sessions. The problem is extremely delicate. On the one hand, such sessions bring together delegates from Churches which are aware that the sole reason for their separation is the lack of contact between them except at such sessions. It may be desirable that these

Churches should give the lie to their divisions, on the occasion of ecumenical sessions, and thus show up their artificiality.[29] But from another point of view such sessions bring together also delegates from Churches which are effectively and consciously divided; they supply definite evidence of the fact that the Church is not one and that they must not treat this division lightly. To experience total intercommunion then appears to me to be very dangerous to ecclesiology, for when Christians communicate together they are proclaiming and practising Christian ecclesiality at its greatest depth. Now such an action can only be temporary and sporadic. If one engages in it nevertheless, there is a risk of implying that the Church herself is only the Church sporadically through what she is doing and not permanently through what she is; there is a risk of suggesting that, when the World Council of Churches is officially assembled, it is the true Church because it celebrates the Eucharist for all and with all. The World Council would thus find itself being led finally to make up for the absence of the one Church by itself becoming this One Church through the event of its communal Eucharist, and this would be the most dangerous short-circuiting of the quest for unity in the Church.[30] So then, if it is desirable that there should be a service of "open" communion at the time of ecumenical sessions to help certain ecclesial families to re-discover each other, to use this as a field for experiments in automatic intercommunion would finally bring about a confusion more danger-ous to unity itself than the sorrowful admission that at least for the time being disunity has to be faced.

Finally, I wonder whether transient and controlled experiments of intercommunion could not be attempted, quite usefully, in the form of practical exercises in unity as it was defined by the Third General Assembly of the World Council of Churches at New Delhi in the autumn of 1961: that all the parishes in a town where there are a large number of confessional Churches should be invited by those under whose authority they are to form together, for an experimental period fixed in advance, the Church of that place, each parish (after eventual territorial regroupings) then becoming a parish of this local Church, superseding the earlier confessional divisions. Such "intercommunion workshops", which could at the same time become "mission work-shops", would perhaps reveal lines of demarcation in places where their existence is not suspected and, on the contrary, profound agreement in places where the opposition had seemed the most marked. They would afford to the Churches which had given a "denominational holiday" to their parishes in this town experiences which would be certainly useful and perhaps even necessary to their quest for unity.

But whatever the result of such attempts, they will not resolve the problem. Intercommunion is certainly not the solution to the healing of the divisions in the Church, but rather communion. I have no doubt in my own mind that the Orthodox Church has the clearest vision on this subject. It is the same as in the ancient eucharistic liturgy; it is *before* the communion that the kiss of peace is exchanged. Let the command of Jesus be remembered, which was linked with fraternal communion in the Supper from the time when the Didache was edited (14: 2 f.) "If you are offering your gift at the altar, and there remember that your brother has something against you, leave your gift there before the altar and go; first be reconciled to your brother, and then come and offer your gift" (Matt. 5: 23 f.).

NOTES

[1] κολλάομαι in 1 Cor. 6: 17 is a verb which denotes extremely close physical unity (cf. 1 Cor. 6: 16; Matt. 19: 5; Gen. 2: 24 LXX (προσκολλάομαι) Acts 5: 13; 9: 26; 17: 34, etc.)

[2] The apostle Paul stresses the idea of communion *in* Christ rather than *with* Christ. But the fact that he reports the institution of the Supper as a meal eaten by Jesus *with* His disciples shows that he bases the second aspect of communion of Christ-Church on the former.

[3] Mark 16: 14; Luke 24: 30 ff., 41 f.; John 21: 9 ff. cf. συναλίζεσθαι of Acts 1: 4.

[4] After quoting Isa. 61: 10, Augustine continues: "Unus videtur loqui, et sponsum se fecit et sponsam se fecit; quia non duo, sed una caro; quia Verbum factum est, et habitavit in nobis. Illi carni adiungitur Ecclesia, et fit Christus totus, caput et corpus." (*Commentary on the First Epistle of John, Sources chrétiennes*, No. 75, Paris, 1961, p. 116.)

[5] John 6: 56. The eucharistic character of at least vv. 51b to 58 in chapter 6 of John's Gospel is hardly now disputed. A comparison of this text of John 6: 56 with 14: 10 would suggest that for the writer of the Fourth Gospel, the sacramental union of Christ with the communicants is comparable to the union of Father and Son. Cod. Cant. interpreted John 6: 56 by the addition of the words: καθὼς ἐν ἐμοὶ ὁ πατὴρ κ᾽αγὼ ἐν τῷ πατρί. Ἀμήν ἀμὴν λέγω ὑμῖν, ἐὰν μὴ λάβητε το σῶμα (!) τοῦ υἱοῦ τοῦ ἀνθρώπου ὡς τὸν ἄρτον τῆς ζωῆς, οὐκ ἔχετε ζωὴν ἐν αὐτῷ

[6] Ph. H. Menoud, *La vie de l'Eglise naissante*, Neuchâtel & Paris, 1952, p. 41.

[7] *Petit traité de la sainte cène*, p. 111, *Trois traités*, Paris, 1934.

[8] Texts like the following come to mind: "By eating the limbs of the Bridegroom and drinking His blood, we achieve a nuptial communion, and κοινωνία (Theodoret of Cyrus, MPG, LXXXI, 128b) or: "Christ gave to the sons of the

bride-chamber the enjoyment of His body and blood" (Cyril of Jerusalem, MPG, XXIII, 1100a). Such quotations could be multiplied.

[9] The Song of Songs which plays a very important part in this interpretation will continue increasingly to be a book read and commented upon by *monks*, that is by men who seek to live under the highest standards of Christian discipleship. On this topic it is noteworthy that for the Jews (who were not allowed to study it before the age of thirty) it formed part of the *Passover* liturgy.

[10] In his *Homilies on Exodus*, Origen states: "No one can ... listen to the Word of God if he has not previously been sanctified, that is, if he is not holy in body and spirit, if he has not washed his garments. In a few minutes' time he is going in to the nuptial banquet, he is going to eat the flesh of the Lamb and to drink the cup of salvation. Let no one go in to this banquet with soiled garments." (*Sources chrétiennes*, No. 16, Paris, 1947, p. 243.)

[11] Notice should be taken in this nuptial and at the same time sacramental perspective how John's Gospel relates the death of Christ (19: 33–37): it is "overprinted" on the story of the creation of Eve (Gen. 2: 21 ff.) and from it flow the sacraments which create and sustain the Church.

[12] Quoted by H. Lietzmann, *op. cit.*, p. 105.

[13] Quoted *ibid.*, pp. 243 f.

[14] Rom. 16: 16; 1 Cor. 16: 20; 2 Cor. 13: 12; 1 Thess. 5: 26; 1 Pet. 5: 14. Was it because the order to exchange the eucharistic kiss of peace goes back to Jesus Himself, that the texts recorded the strong shock felt when Judas betrayed Jesus with a kiss (Luke 22: 48)?

[15] What would remain of the discourse of Jesus on the Bread of Life if one found fault with what is said about communion by eating?

[16] Doubtless a paschal meal or one at least dictated by Jewish paschal usage. But as far as the Agape is concerned, the paschal character of this meal is not important; the important thing was the meal itself.

[17] In the New Testament there is a synonymity between gathering for worship and eating (συνέρχεσθαι εἰς τὸ φαγεῖν 1 Cor. 11: 33) or breaking of bread (συνάγεσθαι κλάσαι ἄρτον Acts 20: 7). Now the ancient notion of table-fellowship presumes that only brethren admitted to the Eucharist were also admitted to the Agape (cf. e.g. 1 Cor. 5: 10 f.; Acts 11: 3; Gen. 43: 32, etc.)

[18] These communal meals were first called "Agapes" in Jude 12 (cf. 2 Peter 2: 13) who complains about them for the same reason which distressed Paul at Corinth.

[19] It was on the meals taken in common that the growth of the Church of Jerusalem threw a very heavy load (cf. Acts 6: 1 ff.). In briefest outline, there arose in the first century a movement, which was to recur in the fourth century, which concerned the structure of the Church's unity in an age marked by a numerical increase. After certain experiments the same decision was taken in both situations to avoid the fragmentation of the Church into congregations existing side by side, which constitutes a threat to Christian unity: in the first century by detaching the Eucharist from the Agape, in the fourth century by refusing to turn each congregation into a Church headed by a bishop, and instead by forming a parish entrusted to a presbyter to whom was delegated a certain number of episcopal prerogatives.

[20] *La liturgie des premiers siècles*, Lex orandi, No. 33, Paris, 1962, p. 66.

[21] To take an example: it is beyond dispute that in the New Testament there is a christology of Jesus–Prophet; but the New Testament itself admits that it is too short to describe the person and the work of Jesus Christ. In a way it would be a rejection of the canonicity of the New Testament if one were to attempt to revive this prophetic christology as a satisfactory interpretation just because it is biblical.

[22] In this context, too, the eucharistic fast ought to be reintroduced.

[23] It is well known that the Church is not divided at the lay level (by baptism) but at the clerical level (by ordination).

[24] Nevertheless, it remains true that certain of these divisions are still necessary. But to know which are necessary, the motives which lie behind must constantly be tested.

[25] Tribute must be paid here to an event of tremendous importance which occurred when the English non-Roman Churches hopefully set the date 1980 for the achievement of union.

[26] In a context where there has been a question of nuptial communion, may I be allowed to use a comparison which comes from the life of an engaged couple. Parents who approve the marriage plans made by their children (and all the Churches belonging to the World Council as well as that of Rome are, in respect to unity between denominations, in the position of parents who approve *nolentes volentes* the marriage plans of their children) only have the right to expect them to remain virgins before their marriage if they help them to get married without delay, otherwise they will have to watch them spend the first years of their married life in conditions quite different from those which formerly made a "good" marriage. On the other hand, it must be admitted that fiancés who have vowed to come to their marriage as virgins generally get married sooner because their passions are more enflamed than fiancés who can afford to wait because they sleep together. I sometimes wonder, however, whether we *love* the Lutherans, the Anglicans, the Orthodox, the Methodists, the Romans, enough to be aflame with desire to share with them the communion table; I also wonder whether our commitment to Christ is deep and radiant enough to make them burn with desire to share with us the Lord's Table.

[27] This is the answer generally given by the Orthodox Churches; but it is possible that if this is the answer they give, it arises from the fact that their ecclesiastical reflexes and their theological thought do not yet really make room for the denominational pluralism which in other areas of Christendom one is forced, by history or the present situation, to take into serious consideration as the temporary situation in which Christian obedience is practised.

[28] The problem of "intercelebration", that is, of the authority to preside over the Eucharist in another confessional Church than that of which one is a minister, raises the same problems and at the same time makes them more complex.

[29] It must be stated, however, that this lack of contact is only true between Churches in countries where there are few denominations. In a situation where there are many denominations, the Church from which, to one's surprise, one is separated will appear to be a totally different Church.

[30] "The Fourth World Faith and Order Conference, Montreal 1963" in the report on Section V, No. 35, states emphatically that the World Council is not the Church because "it does not administer the sacraments and has no ordained ministry" (*Faith and Life*, No. 1, 1964, p. 17).

IV

LIVING BREAD AND SACRIFICE

THE TWO ASPECTS of the eucharistic happening to which this chapter is devoted deal with what might be called the internal movement of the Supper, the dialectic between what comes from God and what is offered to Him. It is particularly around this theme that the conflicts which divide the Church gather; it is on this theme too that a member of the Reformed Church feels least at ease.[1] It is hoped that this confessional difficulty will be appreciated and that what follows will be read for its true value: an attempt at understanding and an invitation to dialogue.

The first part of this chapter will give an account of the Supper as a gift of Living Bread and will deal with these four points: the New Testament terminology used to describe the Supper; the rules to be followed in order to establish the proper relationship between the Eucharist understood as a gift of Living Bread and the meaning of this fact; the mystery which converts this meal into the Lord's meal; and the effects of the Supper.

The New Testament writers do not shrink from using very weighty terms to describe the bread and wine of the Supper.[2] "This is my body, this is my blood", said Jesus on the occasion of the Institution (Mark 14: 22 ff. and par.; 1 Cor. 11: 24 f.).[3] The Apostle Paul speaks without the slightest reticence of "participation in the body and blood of Christ" (1 Cor. 10: 16). The Fourth Gospel attributes to Jesus words which accentuate the sacramental realism as if deliberately to scandalize the Jews (6: 51–71); and goes so far as to establish a causal link between the consumption of the eucharistic species and the gift of salvation: "he who eats my flesh and drinks my blood has eternal life and I will raise him up at the last day . . . he who eats this bread will live for ever" (6: 54, 58). Calvin does not really go beyond the limits of biblical teaching when he states in his *Petit traité de la sainte cène* that "Jesus Christ is the matter and substance of the sacraments".[4]

75

But New Testament eucharistic terminology goes even further than that. The commonly used expression "breaking of bread" may be an indication that the Supper, for all those who took part in it, might sometimes comprise bread alone as eucharistic food. But it seems to be rather a term which is designedly neutral, concealing the fact that the Church's typical meal is a meal for eternal life. The term κοινωνία was analysed in the previous chapter. There are three other expressions used which enable us to grasp the interpretation which the new-born Church placed upon the Supper: manna, spiritual food, and ἐπιούσιος bread.

For the Second Exodus, which would be led by the Messiah, the Jews were expecting a new manna, of which that given in the wilderness was but the foretaste and prefiguration. This expectation is apparent in 1 Corinthians 10: 3 and Revelation 2: 17 where the "hidden manna" presumably refers to the Eucharist, and most of all in the Gospel of John (6: 31, 49). This manna is the food for the last days and enables those who eat it to live for ever. It replaces the manna of the First Exodus and also the bread which Jesus multiplied. This manna is Jesus Himself, "the bread from Heaven", "the bread of God which gives life to the world", "bread of life", or "living bread" which makes us stronger than death and which, now that Jesus has surrendered His body to give eternal life to the cosmos, is communicated and received in the Church through the eucharistic elements "body and blood of the Son of Man".

The theology of the manna thus enables us to understand the Supper as the gift of Living Bread to those who believe in Jesus Christ. The formula used at the distribution of the bread as related by Hippolytus in his *Apostolic Tradition* is interesting: "The bread of heaven in Jesus Christ". But the reference made by the Apostle Paul to manna in 1 Corinthians 10: 1–22 shows that manna may also bring judgment if one does not recognize it for what it is (see also 1 Cor. 11: 27 ff.), or if one imagines that one can partake of it without first renouncing every alleged bread of life of pagan origin. If the generation of the desert is dead it was not—here the Pauline and Johannine theologies part company—because of the powerlessness of the food and drink given by God (was not Christ the Rock from which Israel drank, 1 Cor. 10: 4?), but because they would not rely solely upon this manna to supply their needs.

Speaking of the "supper" of the Exodus, the Apostle uses the expressions of spiritual food and drink (βρῶμα πνευματικόν, πόμα

76

πνευματικόν, 1 Cor. 10: 3 f.).[5] E. Käsemann is very rightly of the opinion that this is a eucharistic terminology earlier than Paul and used by him without hesitation or alteration. The meaning of this adjective has given rise to a number of interpretations. Starting from the Pauline affirmation that the Lord is the Spirit (2 Cor. 3: 17), one may suppose that, because it is spiritual, this food conveys and imparts the Lord who is Spirit and thus the glorified Christ. This is how Käsemann understands it. One may also think of a "pneumatization" of the food (we shall come back to this), or of a kind of resurrected bread which has become spiritual as the bodies of resurrected believers will be spiritual (1 Cor. 15: 44), and consequently of a food which sustains and enlarges the life of those who are raised in Christ at their baptism (spiritual being understood as the opposite, not of material, but of carnal): a food conveying new, eschatological life.

The final expression I should like to mention is also the most mysterious. It is the adjective ἐπιούσιος, which in the Lord's Prayer qualifies the bread for which the Church begs "today". It was probably specially made up for the Greek translation of the Lord's Prayer, for it is unknown before or in any other context, and it is at the same time too ambiguous and too complex to have been proposed haphazardly. Where was this word made up? At Jerusalem among the Hellenists? At Antioch? What expression did Jesus use when He taught His disciples the Prayer? *Machar* meaning "for tomorrow", "for the future" (cf. e.g. Joshua 4: 6), as the Gospel of the Hebrews suggests, or *Thamid* meaning "lasting for ever, perpetual", as certain Syriac versions presuppose and as seems to be allowed in the version of Luke 11: 3, where σήμερον is replaced by τὸ καθ᾽ ἡμέραν meaning "according to the day"? Now this expression καθ᾽ ἡμέραν is found in the LXX where it translates *Thamid* in Numbers 4: 16 and means not so much "for each day" as "regular, habitual,[6] perpetual" according to the sense of the sacrificial terminology of the Old Testament.

But the questions do not stop there. At what point in His ministry did Jesus teach His disciples the Christian Prayer, for Matthew and Luke do not agree on this issue? What is the meaning of "our" bread, namely the bread of those who dare to call God "our Father"? Why is this prayer not reported in the Fourth Gospel where, instead, we have a dialogue between Jesus and those who, not knowing what they were saying, kept asking Him to give them the "bread of God"? To which His reply was "I am the bread of life" (6: 33 ff.; cf. 4: 15). And if one follows the track of this word in the ancient versions of the

Gospels, in the catechesis of the Fathers, or in the liturgical life, questions never cease.

Why did not the Lord's Prayer form part of the elementary catechesis in the great catechetical tradition; was it just the prayer of the baptized —and so of the communicants (which presupposes a link between adoption in Christ which enables one to address God as Father and the content of what one asks of Him)? Why do the Fathers so readily see in this expression a reference to the Eucharist? Why did the Latin translators hesitate between *quotidianus* (Itala, retained by the Vulgate for Luke 11: 3) and *supersubstantialis* (Jerome, retained by the Vulgate for Matt. 6: 11), and why does the ordinary meaning of daily bread, that is a basic minimum for subsistence, indicate so inadequately the oldest tradition, before the weakening of the eschatological awareness of Christians in the new sociological situation in which the Church was set from the fourth century on?

The accumulation of these questions and the answer which they suggest leads us to think that the fourth petition of the Lord's Prayer says in brief: "Give us today (already, right now), the bread of eternal life". This ἐπιούσιος bread is indeed described in three ways: it is no more at man's disposal than are the sanctification of God's Name, the coming of His Kingdom, the fulfilment of His Will, pardon for sins, protection against the great final tribulation and deliverance from all the assaults of the Evil One: it can only be given by God, it can only be an answer to prayer. This bread is described also as bread of the future (if ἐπιούσιος is derived from ἐπιέναι) or finally as a "super-substantial" bread, multiplied by means of a virtue lacking in ordinary bread (if ἐπιούσιος comes from ἐπεῖναι). It must then be the bread of the Supper.

All the expressions listed agree entirely in saying that the living Christ is present at the Supper, that in the Supper we feed on "the bread of the Lord which is sanctified to represent for us and to dispense to us the body of Christ", as Calvin says.[7] The Supper, in biblical terminology, is a Resurrection meal, the Sunday meal shared by those who have been born again by water and the Spirit. There are no grounds for imputing a non-biblical inspiration to Ignatius of Antioch when he described the Supper as an "elixir of immortality, an antidote against death, giving eternal life in Jesus" (φάρμακον ἀθανασίας, ἀντίδοτος τοῦ μὴ ἀποθανεῖν, ἀλλὰ ζῆν ἐν 'Ιησοῦ διὰ πάντος, Eph. 20: 2) even if the Christian origin of the formula φάρμακον ἀθανασίας is open to debate.[8]

By means of the eucharistic meal the living Lord nourishes His own for life eternal. Through the bread and wine, He gives Himself to them as food for eternity. That is the fact. To establish the relationship between the fact and its significance, three rules must be observed.

(1) As in every branch of Christian theology, eucharistic theology is first of all an *act* of adoration in which thought, however exacting and critical it may be, is transformed into an offering. This liturgical interpretation of theology does not exempt it, here or elsewhere, from the duty of giving a reasonable account of the fact, the significance of which is to be sought; but this interpretation rules out any claim to reach such a grasp of the fact as would put it at the disposition of anyone who had penetrated its "mechanism". For there are only two intentions in eucharistic theology: to protect the Supper from the two threats which constantly menace it, magic and symbolism; and to help believers to rejoice in the bread of life that Christ gives because He gives Himself therein.

(2) One must avoid such a close coincidence between the fact and its interpretation that it becomes no longer possible to differentiate between them, so that the fact is tied to the one interpretation which has been assigned to it and so that the interpretation involves the fact in its own fate. The history of eucharistic theology proves conclusively that theologians must operate here with philosophical concepts. Now these are not immutable. Consequently, one must avoid the temptation to "modernize" eucharistic theology, that is to say, impose upon it a unique and exclusive interpretation (even if at a certain epoch this seems the best interpretation), otherwise one runs the risk, either of artificially perpetuating the officially approved interpretation which would make of the Church's greatness something belonging to a *former* age, whereas she must always encounter the human today in the light of the age *to come*, or of rejecting the accepted interpretation, which carries with it a rejection of the fact itself or which at least does harm to the fact.

It is impossible to overestimate what the Church has lost by gradually relinquishing the wealth and variety of the eucharistic language of the Early Church. Morever, this impoverishment has produced a kind of unwitting protest of the favoured interpretation against the honour given to it, as though the Church shrank from being left alone with the mystery which she was supposed to disclose.

In view of the liturgical attitude just mentioned, a theology of the Eucharist could never dominate but on the contrary must celebrate the eucharistic fact. It cannot be compared to a pass in wrestling which, seeming to be the right one, encourages us to scorn all others because it enables us to get a grip on our opponent and throw him to the ground. It is true that the "theological celebration" approach brings about a certain differentiation between formulations which swing clearly towards the element of mystery and those which definitely swing away from it; but this differentiation must be singularly conservative. I think that it can be argued that if in the eucharistic theology of the West (and the practice resulting from it) there had not been a narrow mistrust of the eucharistic theologies current in the early Church, the protest of the Reformation might have been avoided.

(3) The liturgical approach which dominates eucharistic theology is imposed by the eucharistic fact itself. This cannot be spirited away or denuded of its power, nor can its factual reality be questioned. To call into question its factual reality under the pretext that it might threaten the uniqueness of Christ is tantamount to accusing the Lord of being unaware of what He was risking when He instituted the Supper. And to question it on the pretext that what the Supper claims to be (the Real Presence of the glorified Christ among His own) and to do (impart Christ as food for life eternal) is a piece of scandalous folly; this is to prejudge the fact in favour of an interpretation, also officially accepted, which ties up, but in the opposite way, with what we have just observed. One starts then from the principle that the Supper cannot be what it claims to be and no convincing reason for its celebration is apparent since its celebration only has meaning if it is what it claims to be. To admit that it is still celebrated because a command of Christ must be obeyed is decidedly weak, since it is evident that Jesus did not institute the Supper just for the pleasure of establishing a rite and giving an order. He was neither a religious aesthete nor a tyrant.

But how does the Supper become this meal for life eternal?

When we were speaking of the epiklesis, we saw that there are two traditional answers. They are not mutually exclusive, and it is when their opposition is exaggerated that they can pass summarily for eastern and western.

The first, which we shall call "eastern", claims that the miracle is the work of the Holy Spirit, invoked upon the elements and upon the Church to make of them the Body of Christ. The situation is reminiscent of certain scenes in the Old Testament, for example, on Carmel, when Elijah, after he had made all arrangements for the sacrifice, called upon

God to intervene personally to make the sacrifice effective (1 Kings 18: 22–40; cf. Gen. 15: 9 ff., 17; Judges 6: 17–24). What characterizes this response is the attention which it focuses, not only upon the elements which have been prepared, but on the people who also have been prepared, by baptism and by the preaching of the Gospel, and, consequently, the "transformation" into the Body of Christ involves, not merely the bread and wine, but also the assembled people.

The second answer, which we shall call the "western", claims that the eucharistic miracle is the work of the Word of God, active and powerful. When it has access to the elements, it enables the sacrament to come into being.[9] This view is also that of the Reformers. For example, in chapter 19 of *La Confession helvétique postérieure*, H. Bullinger says, "that which was not sacrament is made sacrament by the Word of God, more especially as it is consecrated by the Word and declared sanctified by Him who ordained it".[10] Here the situation is that of the Gospel scenes where Jesus touched the eyes of a blind man and made him see, the tongue of a mute and made him shout aloud in praise, the coffin of a dead man and brought him to life.[11] The feature of this view, independently of the theological "dress" it wears, is that its emphasis falls primarily on the elements which alone are "transformed". The Church is only "transformed" indirectly, *a posteriori* in so far as she partakes of the body and blood of Christ. In principle this answer assumes more than does the former that the people must communicate for there to be a real Eucharist.

Is it permissible to go further and to say what takes place at the moment when the Spirit responds by His intervention, when the Word acts? One can only stammer, fumble, wonder, and perhaps make use of two types of biblical reference to illustrate the eucharistic "metabolism".[12] The first is the mystery of the Incarnation. One might say that at the moment of the Eucharist something occurs like an echo of what happened when the Word was made flesh. If I understand aright, it was Justin Martyr who first looked for a solution in this direction.[13] It is interesting because it may enable us to understand more easily why the discourse of Jesus on the Bread of Life, in places so brutally shocking, ends with the words, "It is the Spirit that gives life, the flesh is of no avail" (John 6: 63). It was the same with the Incarnation where the important thing was that it was the Word which became flesh and wherein, without the Word, the flesh would have served no purpose.

The second reference is the mystery of the resurrection. If I understand aright, it was St. Irenaeus who was the first to look for a solution in this direction.[14] Then the Supper would be a mystery quite proper to the first day of the week; the "supernatural food" of 1 Corinthians 10: 3 ought then to be understood as a resurrection process parallel to that of the "spiritual body" of 1 Corinthians 15: 44; it would through the power of the Spirit become a "resurrected" food, "supersubstantial", thus capable of becoming resurrection food (to use one of the most frequent expressions in the eucharistic terminology of the Fathers).

These can only be very tentative hypotheses. In comparison with the biblical evidence, one thing, however, it seems to me, can be accepted as a thesis: the eucharistic species at the time of the Eucharist are charged with eschatological power, they are food and drink of the Spirit and so of life, and it is not possible to detach this power from the elements which convey it.

Perhaps at this point the problem of the one who presides over the eucharistic assembly is most sharply presented. If the Supper is what we have understood it to be, it is evident that authority must be given to preside over it just as authority is given to take part in it. Too often it is forgotten that the question of the official recognition of the one who presides over the Supper is parallel to the official recognition of the communicants at the Supper. The Supper being the fundamental test in the discipline of the baptized—shall they be admitted to the Lord's Table or excluded from it?—one must not be offended if it is also the fundamental test in the discipline which governs the exercise of the sacred ministry. A true minister of Christ is one whose right to preside in Christ's name over the eucharistic assembly is not questioned, in the same way that a true member of Christ's Church is one whose right to join in the worship and the communion on the occasion of this assembly is not questioned.

The problem of the official recognition of a man for the sacred ministry would lose a good deal of its annoying, disagreeable, tiresomely "clerical", aspects, if one looked at it as parallel to that of the recognition of the laity and of their right to take communion. It would then be understood more clearly why those who usurp a ministry so charged with authority[15] should be removed, and removed as a result of a reflex as prompt and unconditional as that of Simon Peter when he condemned Simon Magus (Acts 8: 20 ff.). The People of God must have full confidence in the one who claims to act in Christ's name and be assured that what they receive at the Lord's Table is indeed the

Bread of Life, because the one who prepares and distributes it has the right to do so.

This does not in any sense mean that this right can become for the minister any other kind of right than that of serving Christ. This was why, on the occasion of the Donatist controversy, the Church rejected the idea that the efficacy of the Eucharist should be *opus operantis*, the work of him who presides over it, as if by the celebration of the Supper the minister had control of God and His intervention. This rejection does not mean either that whoever is the *operans* the Supper will be a meal conveying life *ex opere operato*, by the mere fact of having been celebrated. If the reality of the eucharistic happening depends on the intervention of God and not on the power of men, this does not undermine the necessity for ministers of Christ in and for the Church.[16]

If now we try to enumerate the results of the eucharistic communion, what we have already seen supplies the essential answer: the communion is related to the eternal salvation of the communicants. Being κοινωνία, communion in the body and blood of Christ, it integrates the communicant into Christ who gives Himself for the world's salvation; as it involves feeding on Christ (John 6: 57) who is the resurrection and the life, it conveys to the worshipper a post-judgment life, life eternal. In the Reformed Church, where we have not forgotten how reluctant Zwingli was to establish a link between communion and salvation, it is nevertheless well worth while dwelling on this question to find out whether it can be admitted with Calvin that in the Supper "Jesus Christ is offered . . . to us, so that we may possess Him, and in Him all the fullness of grace that we may desire".[17]

The relation between communion and salvation is first apparent negatively in the fact that the Supper is for the Christian community a kind of anticipation of the Last Judgment. To communicate is not for them an automatic guarantee of salvation. St. Paul first stated this. He envisaged the Supper as food which threatened with perdition those for whom the eucharistic communion did not inhibit participation in other, in false "supersubstantial" promises of life. In his writings, one finds the same all-out struggle which the Prophets waged in defence of the exclusive nature of the worship of Yahweh: under the threat of the penalty of death one may not seek fullness of vitality in the union of Spirit with Christ and in a carnal union with a (sacred?) prostitute (1 Cor. 6: 12–20) or look for a food stronger than death at the table of the Lord and at that of the demons (1 Cor. 10: 6, 22).

As the Israelites died in the wilderness because of their religious duplicity, their idolatry, their orgies even when they had been baptized in Moses and had partaken of spiritual food and drink, so Christians too, although baptized and communicants, could still die beneath divine condemnation (compare 1 Cor. 10: 1–13; 11: 30 ff.). Even more, the communion can become a source of condemnation for those who participate in it without knowing what they are doing,[18] because they make themselves guilty towards the Lord's body and blood, that is to say, they enter into league with those who, being more ignorant of what they were doing, carried their opposition to the will of Jesus to the point of putting Him to death.

In response to His love, Jesus expects an exclusive love[19] from His followers, otherwise the Supper becomes a judgment of Christ upon the offender (doubtless so that the whole Church "may not be condemned along with the world" (1 Cor. 11: 32)).[20] For those who celebrate the communion without realizing that it is the Lord's Supper (1 Cor. 11: 20) they are celebrating, it then becomes what one is tempted to call a $\phi\acute{\alpha}\rho\mu\alpha\kappa\text{o}\nu$ $\theta\alpha\nu\acute{\alpha}\tau\text{o}\nu$. It is this which enables us to understand to some extent why, from the fourth century especially, participation in the communion became less regular because it frightened people—an attitude the very reverse of Paul's, whose appreciation of the specific nature of the Supper led him to advocate participation in it.

But the results of the Supper are primarily and essentially positive. The Supper brings forgiveness of, and freedom from the hold of, sin. Luther repeatedly stressed the power of the Supper to purify those who take part: "Was ist den nu diss testament oder was wirt uns drynnen bescheyden von Christo? fur war ein grosser ewiger, unaussprechlicher schatz, nemlich vorgebung aller sund".[21] But the Supper has more than just this polemical aspect. It is the food and drink of eternal life, that is to say, it strengthens the new man in the baptized person and makes him grow, it contributes to his transformation and glorification (cf. 2 Cor. 3: 18). Consequently, it helps this new man to impose his presence on the old man, and so is a factor in sanctification.

Even more than this, it gradually acclimatizes believers to the life of the world to come. "This body which proved stronger than death and which for us has become the source of life", to use the words of a catechetical discourse of Gregory of Nyssa,[22] given in the bread and wine of the Supper, involves those who receive it in the mechanism of its own glorification, and consequently confers upon the Church, right in the midst of this world whose burden and limitations she knows only too well, the privilege of being an eschatological people, the body of the Risen Christ.

A post-communion prayer from the Clementine liturgy summed up the effects of the communion in the words: "Having received the precious body and blood of Christ, let us give thanks to Him for having shared in His holy mysteries and let us ask Him that this shall be not for our condemnation but for our salvation, for the good of our souls and bodies, for the remission of our sins, for the life of the age to come".[23] We need not hesitate to accept this as a faithful paraphrase of the words of Jesus: "He who eats my flesh and drinks my blood has eternal life and I will raise him up at the last day . . . He who eats my flesh and drinks my blood abides in me, and I in him. As the living Father sent me, and I live because of the Father, so he who eats me will live because of me" (John 6: 54 f.).

Now the Supper is all this within a framework which transcends the personal life of the communicants. First, because the celebration of the Supper constitutes the Church as the Body of Christ, as has been emphasized earlier; then, because the Supper is mysteriously linked with the history of the world. It creates, at the command of Christ, the anamnesis of His death and resurrection, and consequently incorporates those who celebrate it into the decisive, culminating moment in the history of the world's salvation. It is impossible to celebrate the Supper without being aware that it concerns the history of the world, or to proclaim the death and resurrection of Christ without knowing that they affect, first and foremost and in a vital sense, the whole world. Even when celebrated in a hole and corner, behind closed doors, the Supper is still a political action which, we must repeat, advances the history of salvation and sets in motion the Church and the world towards the day when the Kingdom will come.

If the Lord's Supper really is the meal which confers eternal life, two questions must be faced. The first is addressed to the Roman Catholic Church and those who, on this point, try to imitate her: what purpose can "transubstantiation" serve if the Eucharist can be validly celebrated without the communion of the people, if the bread which has become bread of life is not on each occasion distributed to those baptized people present so that they can abide in the new life, continue to grow in it, and testify to it when they return to the world?

The second question is addressed to the Reformed Church and to those who, on this issue, take the same line: who could possibly have given to those responsible for the Church the right to celebrate Sunday without celebrating the Eucharist and as a result to deprive the Christian people of the meal through which Christ seeks to dwell in each of His members and give them life?

There is still another question which must be put to all the Churches. Has not the time come for us to make a joint re-assessment of the Supper, to make together an inventory of the antitheses, the misunderstandings, the distortions, positive and negative, which divide the Church on the subject of eucharistic doctrine and practice, to question each other, in a spirit of willingness to listen to the answers of the others instead of trying to formulate them ourselves, on what Christians of each confessional tradition basically intend when they celebrate the Supper as they do. Exegetical research, liturgical and patristic knowledge are sufficiently shared among the various Churches for the time to be apparently ripe. And, above all, there is this sense of being tired of divisions based on grounds which have not been confirmed by a recent study in depth, this weariness of divisions which some see as a dangerous temptation, whereas it is really an immense source of hope.

The aim of this chapter is to speak about the movement of the Supper, the dialectic between what comes from God when it is celebrated and what goes up to Him. Having acknowledged "the bread of God which comes down from heaven and gives life to the world" (John 6: 33), we must now speak of the upward movement, the elevatory sacrificial movement. This is to be understood in the context of the movement of the glorification of Christ which, in biblical theology means at one and the same time His elevation on the Cross,[24] His priestly entrance into the heavenly temple,[25] and His continuous intercession on behalf of His own.[26]

The alliance between Supper and sacrifice is so suspect among us that this aspect is even more delicate of approach than that of the Supper-Bread of Life alliance. To find a way out of our difficulties perhaps the simplest thing would be to set out the reasons for Christ's institution of the Supper. Before we can do that two brief preliminary remarks are necessary.

The first is a statement of fact: the whole early Christian tradition, when speaking of the Supper, makes use of a sacrificial terminology. Alan Richardson makes on this subject a claim which is calculated to embarrass us:

In the Church of the Apostolic Fathers and of the ante-Nicene Fathers the Eucharist is everywhere spoken of as a sacrifice. Sacrificial phraseology is habitually employed in connection with it. There are no exceptions to these statements, and it cannot seriously be denied that the Fathers of the ancient Church understood the apostolic tradition of the Eucharist in this way. The burden of proving that their unanimous interpretation of the scriptural evidence was wrong rests upon those who would deny any form of Eucharistic sacrifice. If they were wrong, then we are faced with the quite incredible proposition that all the teachers of the Church from the time of Saint Clement of Rome or Saint Ignatius of Antioch were in error until the true doctrine was revealed to the Protestant reformers.[26a]

It is not absolutely out of the question *a priori* that a Church should be right in face of the entire ancient tradition and in opposition to the overwhelming majority of the other contemporary Churches. But when this does happen, love of truth as well as humility demands that very serious attention should be paid to this unanimity facing us to see whether one can really stand up to this confrontation honestly, or to see if what one is defending against this unanimity cannot be presented in such a way as to be harmonized with the general view—reserving the right to colour it a little differently so that what one is defending single-handed, and perhaps with good reason, should receive greater respect from those who would welcome our acceptance of the general position.[27]

The second observation seems in contradiction to the one just made. It must remain clearly beyond discussion that the sacrifice on Calvary is unique, and is therefore adequate to reconcile God and the world for all time. Jesus died "once for all"; the uniqueness of His death was as exclusive and as sufficient as was His incarnation and as His return will be.[28] If His name is the only name by which the world can be rescued, it is because Christ offered the only sacrifice which could save the world. The Gospel is the declaration of this without reserve or compromise.

But what then was the reason for this unanimity in the way early tradition interpreted the Supper with the help of sacrificial terminology? This question could never have arisen if Jesus had been content to charge His disciples to tell the world that He had died to save mankind. There could then have been no threat to the uniqueness of the Cross. But Jesus, in addition, instituted the Supper and set it in a direct relationship with this unique and all-sufficient death, possibly to become a threat to this uniqueness and to this sufficiency. Why did He do so?

At the outset let us refute three wrong answers to this question.

The first turns on the expression anamnesis, memory or memorial. Jesus would have instituted the Supper so that His sacrifice should not be forgotten by men or (according to the hypothesis of J. Jeremias) by God. It is a mnemonic ceremony. It is as though the passion and victory of Christ had so fallen into oblivion that they were only proclaimed to men and recalled to God's mind in the act of thanksgiving and intercession. This misunderstanding of the anamnesis has already been dismissed in the first chapter; I have come back to it only to emphasize how incomprehensible, arbitrary and entirely unprofitable the order to celebrate the Supper becomes when the anamnesis is interpreted in this way.

A second false answer is given by those who think that, if Jesus did institute something in the nature of the Supper, it was the Agape, and that this was later transformed into the Eucharist, either to find a substitute for the return of Christ which had been promised but surely delayed, or through a doctrinal distortion due to the influence of a paganism (or a Judaism) which they had not shaken off, or for any other reason. I am admittedly somewhat afraid that the revival of the Agape and the hopes it arouses might lead the Church in the direction that this reply suggests, and, finally might cause the Church, in choosing between the Agape and the Supper, to come down in favour of the Agape. This would at the same time supply the opportunity, not to say the relief, of exchanging the harsh doctrinal realities of the Eucharist for satisfying engagement in social service. But we saw in Chapter III that, if the communal meals eaten with Jesus played a certain part in the eucharistic context of the infant Church, and if the Eucharist, being a fraternal communion, inevitably overflows in service, it was not the Agape that Jesus instituted on the night when He was delivered up.

A third false answer spread first in the "catholic", then in the "protestant", tradition under the pressure of dualistic philosophies. Jesus would have instituted the Supper to make faith easier for us, because we are so ensnared in matter that He had to have recourse to temporary, pedagogic concessions to release us from it. The Supper then would be one of the concessions.

Two arguments can be brought against this. The first is based on the very grounds of the statement made: Christian sacramentalism, as is proved in particular by the Gnostic temptation which recurs in the Church, is more of a stumbling block to the natural man than the antimaterialism into which his purest desires impel him. We would ask for nothing better than to dispense with the sacraments since they remind us emphatically that God's purpose is not to save us from the world but to save the world. P. Benoît expresses this well when he says:

> If the Word took a human body, it was not merely to communicate with men on the plane of his senses. It was more particularly that he might take in hand the whole man, body and soul, and remake him wholly, body and soul . . . so when He communicates His life to His followers, it is their bodies as well as their souls that He joins to Himself that He may re-create them. It is His body as well as His soul that He brings into contact with theirs to enable them to share in His "passage" from death to life.[29]

The second argument is specifically Christian. If Jesus Christ really instituted the holy Supper because of our deplorable carnality, one would not understand why the whole apostolic teaching informs us that the Supper is destined not for the old man but for the *new* man, that in order to communicate one must be baptized and live according to the baptismal resurrection, that it is not carnal food, a $\beta\rho\hat{\omega}\mu\alpha$ $\sigma\alpha\rho\kappa\iota\kappa\acute{o}\nu$ but spiritual food, a $\beta\rho\hat{\omega}\mu\alpha$ $\pi\nu\epsilon\upsilon\mu\alpha\tau\iota\kappa\acute{o}\nu$.

So then, is it known why Jesus instituted the Supper? It seems to me that the New Testament puts forward three reasons—soteriological, liturgical and eschatological—which moreover are complementary and overlapping.

First, Jesus instituted the Supper because He interpreted His death as a sacrifice offered to God for the world's salvation. We must start from the conviction that Jesus was aware of Himself as Messiah. I admit that this is to beg the question since those exegetes who question the messianic consciousness of Jesus are still very vocal; but if Jesus did not recognize Himself as Messiah—consciously combining and fulfilling different Old Testament christologies, especially that of the Davidic sonship, of the Son of Man and pre-eminently that of the Servant of Yahweh sacrificed for the sins of others (Isaiah 53)—the Gospel as history seems to me quite unintelligible. It is equally impossible to understand why Jesus underwent the baptism of John, why He never married, why He chose exactly twelve men from among His followers to train them for the future, why He chose to carry out His work on the sabbath day, why He went up to Jerusalem knowing that death threatened Him there, why He instituted the Supper, why He allowed Himself to be arrested so easily. I start then from the natural assumption of the Gospels: Jesus knew that He was the Messiah and gave to His death a messianic significance: the significance of a sacrifice which was decisive for the history of the world.

The indissoluble link between the death of Christ and sacrifice on one hand, and the death of Christ and the Eucharist on the other, explains why the unanimous patristic tradition speaks of the Supper in sacrificial terms. But we must go further: this terminology is that which is found in the New Testament. I am not thinking just of the comparison which Paul, without giving the impression that he was making a μετάβασις εἰς ἄλλο γένος, established between the Christian Supper and the pagan sacrifices (cf. e.g. 1 Cor. 10: 14–22), or of John's silence on the institution of the Supper, implying that it was the sacrificial death of Christ which instituted it. It is striking that the biblical terminology of the Eucharist is full of allusions to sacrifices, especially to that of the paschal lamb—Jesus becoming our Passover sacrifice (1 Cor. 5: 7),[30] to the sacrifice which sealed the Sinai covenant,[31] and to the Sacrifice on Calvary which gathered them all up and fulfilled them. Even the command to repeat the ordinance ("do this") is not without sacrificial connotation.[32]

Understanding His death as the supreme messianic deed, that is, as a sacrifice with power to reconcile God and the world, Jesus instituted in the Supper the memorial of this sacrifice. But it was a memorial in the sense that we have already established: so that by means of this memorial what Jesus did might remain fresh, that those who enact the anamnesis might benefit from this reconciliation through the very anamnesis which they enact, that the history of salvation might continue and develop, that He, the Crucified, might remain present among His followers to give Himself to them in the gift of what He has done for them.[33]

Protestant theologians speak freely of a "sacramental phraseology" which enables us to make identifications by analogy, such as the identification bread-body. One might have recourse to this prudent method of expression and speak of a "sacrificial phraseology" which uses an analogy to describe the Supper as a sacrifice. In any case, this was the sense which the Fathers intended when they used the term sacrifice, knowing full well that it was an unsuitable term, but they used it nevertheless, as though compelled to do so on account of the sacrifice of which the Supper is the anamnesis and because to renounce sacrificial language in this context would have been to separate the Supper from the passion of Christ and to have robbed it of its meaning. That is why, on the one hand, they emphasized the gulf between the eucharistic sacrifice and the Jewish and pagan sacrifices, and, on the other hand, they became more and more accustomed to the use of "sacrificial phraseology" when speaking of the eucharistic life, with the help, however, of certain circumlocutions and certain contradictions in the very terms. Athenagoras, towards 180 A.D., was the first to use the expression προσφορὰ ἀναιμακτός ("unbloody offering") to describe the Supper, that is to say, in terms of a sacrifice which is, and at the same time is not, a sacrifice.

That this terminology should be fraught with danger from the time when the Church was no longer existentially confronted by sacrifices (Jewish or pagan) which enabled her to locate the "eucharistic" sacrifice in a polemical way, is only too true. But that is not a sufficient reason to rule out all sacrificial terminology when speaking of the Supper, for then you deal a blow at the intention of Jesus when He made it a sacrament of His sacrifice. To detach the Supper from its sacrificial references and context is in the last analysis to compromise what attaches it to the death of Christ which was a sacrificial death; at the very least it weakens its significance as an anamnesis.[34]

The second reason why Jesus instituted the Supper was to give His followers an example and a command. This reason must stay in second place, for the Cross can be an example only because it is first of all a work of reconciliation; otherwise it would only be the example of a romantic heroism easily deflated by a little reason, a little prudence, a little timidity. When He instituted the Supper, Jesus gave His disciples the example of what they must be and told them what they must do if they would remain His followers. This is also why it is a vital purpose of the Supper to reunite those who are reconciled, men who love each other.[35] Jesus thus invites His disciples to have "the mind that was in Christ Jesus" (Phil. 2: 5). He invited them through their own sacrifice to share in His sacrifice, He involves and welcomes the Church into His sacrifice. "There is the sacrifice of Christians", St. Augustine was to say, "all together one body in Christ,"[36] and he added that the Church learns this sacrifice on the occasion of the Supper, in which she has seen that in the gift she offers, she herself is offered.[37]

It can be stated then that Jesus instituted the Supper to sum up, to recapitulate and to direct the fundamentally liturgical attitude which baptismal resurrection confers on man, and to lead him to an understanding that in himself he cannot be other than "offerer", a προσφέρων, to use the term employed in the liturgies of St. Basil and

St. John Chrysostom to describe the worshippers at the time of the anamnesis. It is from this angle that one can understand why Jesus (if I may dare to say so) was so little concerned for the uniqueness of His sacrifice—morever Jesus does not distrust His Church, He loves her.

His Cross is unique, but He tells His followers that they must carry theirs.[38] His sufferings have once for all wiped out all sins, but yet they still abound in those who belong to Him and are incorporated in Him.[39] He alone is the Lamb of God who bears and takes away the sin of the world, and yet it is by self-sacrifice that one becomes a Christian,[40] and often the Christian's death is a sacrifice too.[41] A single sacrifice was enough to enable men to rediscover life; at the same time Christians must offer to God their body as a living and holy sacrifice.[42]

The Supper is certainly not the moment at which the Christian bears his cross, suffers for Christ, etc. But since it is not merely the most intense phase of the sacrifice of praise which the Church offers through Christ to God (cf. Hebrews 13: 15), the Supper becomes in a way the channel of the sacrifice of Christians, the sacrament of their sacrifice as it is the sacrament of the sacrifice of Christ. Morever, it is by their identification with Christ offered on the Cross for the reconciliation of the world that all Christian prayers rise, since they are offered in His name.

This has certainly played an important part in the spread of sacrificial terminology applied to the Supper. The Eucharist (this term already carries sacrificial overtones) is the moment when the Church makes an offering of herself, when, if I may dare say so, she rushes towards God through the breach made by the death of Jesus in a heaven otherwise walled up,[43] when she moves forward in procession to give herself in and through what she is bringing with her.[44]

St. Augustine is perfectly right: when she celebrates the sacrifice of Christ, the Church, which is the Body of Christ, learns that she has offered herself in the sacrifice which she is celebrating. I will go so far as to say that the Church must renounce her claims to be the Body of Christ unless she continues to interpret the Supper in a sacrificial way. For the sacrificial element in the Supper applies not only to "the likeness of the death of Christ" ($\tau\grave{o}$ $\acute{o}\mu o\acute{\iota}\omega\mu\alpha$ $\tauο\hat{υ}$ $\theta\alpha\nu\acuteα\tauο\upsilon$ $\pi ο\iota\epsilon\hat{\iota}\nu$), as the Anaphora of Serapion says, which is produced when the bread is broken and the cup of the New Covenant elevated: it applies also to the eucharistic prayers, to the confessions of faith, to the acts of adoration and intercession made in the name of Jesus, and equally to the material offering used to make the Eucharist and to the offertory of those who, to use the words of the Liturgy of St. Basil, "dare to approach the holy altar and present as an offering the antitypes of the sacred body and blood of Christ", of those who in Christ have become a people of kings and priests (Rev. 1: 6).

A third reason for which Jesus instituted the Supper was that the eschatological meal, the meal with Him, should remain central in the Church. This meal acquired for the disciples its significance as a messianic meal after they had recognized Him as the Messiah. We shall come back to this in the next chapter. We refer to it at this point since the Supper certainly owes its institution to Jesus' desire to leave for His followers a living sign of the future of the Kingdom which, in Him, had already ventured into this world. When He instituted the Supper, He was not merely instituting the memorial of His saving sacrifice, not merely offering to His followers the means by which they might, with Him and in Him, celebrate the worship which God expects of them; He was giving them a foretaste of the meal in the expectation of which He Himself fasted on the night when He was betrayed.

When the apostle Paul told the Corinthians that, when they ate this bread and drank this cup, they proclaimed the Lord's death "till He come" (1 Cor. 11: 26), that did not mean that the sacrament of the Supper is only, like that of Baptism, for the period of the Church's existence, and that consequently there would be no Supper in the Kingdom. There are too many promises which speak of being at table in the Kingdom (Mark 14: 25 and par.; Matt. 8: 11; Luke 22: 30), and too many parables which imply it (Matt. 22: 1–14; Luke 14: 15–24; Matt. 25: 1–13, 21, 23; Luke 15: 23, etc.). Paul meant that, until the Parousia, the Supper bears of necessity the double sacrificial element of which we have spoken, but that after the Parousia this sacrificial aspect of the Supper will be superseded and there will then remain only the final reason for which Jesus instituted it: the joy of the present Kingdom shared in the fraternal communion.

One might venture to suggest the following parallel: just as the basic Christian attitude is compounded of faith, hope and love, but love is the sole obligation of Christian living which will survive the Parousia (1 Cor. 13: 8), so the Supper is compounded of anamnesis of the historic sacrifice of Christ, of self-dedication to Christ as the present High Priest, and of anticipation of the messianic meal, but only this last aspect will survive the Parousia because this latter will fulfil the others so completely that they will no longer serve any purpose.[45]

As long as the present age endures, there is no grace that the Evil One will not seek to corrupt. The Supper, in the three senses that we have looked at, is on this account subject to three definite dangers.

The first is to confuse the anamnesis of the death of Christ with the death itself; the temptation, therefore, is not to proclaim the death of Christ, as it were, inside this death but alongside it. Then the Supper will be understood as a repetition of the sacrifice of the Cross, it will be turned into a propitiatory sacrifice in its own right and thus the Gospel will be subverted because the impression is given that, for the sacrifice of Christ not to disappear, not to sink into oblivion, it must be repeated, and the repetitions multiplied *ad infinitum*. It was against this very idea of the Sacrifice of the Mass that the Reformers protested,[46] and the attempts at doctrinal correction which have since been made by Rome prove that this protest was legitimate since it struck home.

The second temptation is to draw the Church away from Jesus' reconciling worship on the Cross or to prevent her from sharing it as the Body of Christ. This also leads to an overthrowing of the Gospel, either because Christ is limited to a sacrificial monopoly so radical that the Church is deprived of all theologically essential reality for the history of salvation, or because the Christian life is ranged not *in* Christ, but *alongside* Him, and thus in a context where it can only take on a sacrificial colouring through its own self-righteousness, if it is not to become paralysed through the renunciation of every sacrificial impulse, of every act of self-dedication for fear of competing with Christ and His exclusive monopoly of self-giving.

The third temptation is to detach the Supper from the first two reasons for its institution, and consequently to detach it both from its obligation as anamnesis of the death of Christ and from the grace which is conferred upon it to enable it to be the bearer of the liturgical life of the Church. Here, too, there results a reversal of the Gospel, either because the Church forgets that she is still in this world and, like the puffed-up Corinthians (1 Cor. 4: 19) takes her ease during the Supper in a glory which she believes to be beyond the danger of a relapse, or because she forgets that the idea of the "natural" meal has not yet replaced that of the "cultic" meal, and the whole of time has not yet been transfigured into Sunday, worship remains necessary as worship,

LIVING BREAD AND SACRIFICE

with the formal rules, the intermittent character, the limitations and the shortcomings which it must share if it is to express all the yearnings of creation.[47]

To understand, as a protestant theologian, the place of the sacrificial aspect of the Eucharist, a certain parallelism may be used between the problem now occupying our attention and the discipline of excommunication.

When the Church excommunicates one of her members, she is purified, but at the same time she feels that she has suffered an amputation and longs for the repentance of the excommunicant so that she may welcome him back into her life.

I wonder whether the theological discipline which must operate in the Church ought not to be interpreted in the same way. A theological concept—the sacrificial character of the Eucharist—claimed for itself in the life of the Church a position which impinges upon other indispensable aspects of eucharistic theology. It then became apparent, at a time when the Church was striving to regain a correct balance in her eucharistic theology, that the sacrificial aspect of this theology had become so obstructive and so imperious that it seemed impossible to reduce it to proportions which would allow other aspects of eucharistic theology to find their place alongside the sacrificial aspect. Provisionally, in order to allow these other aspects to recover the place which had been usurped, it was necessary to "put under discipline", to excommunicate in a way, the sacrificial aspect of this theology. But it was a temporary "act of discipline" because this sacrificial aspect is an integral part of a Christian theology of the Eucharist. Now that the other aspects have recovered their rights, and to prevent them from committing the same error which had been committed by the sacrificial aspect of eucharistic theology, so that they may not occupy more room than rightly belongs to them, the sacrificial aspect must be sought and brought back but only in a state of "penitence", that is, confined to the role which belongs to it so that eucharistic theology should be balanced and harmonious.

Indeed, what we have seen of the Supper as Sacrifice is decisive enough to enable us to say that the Supper suffers the amputation of one of its component elements if it is deprived of its sacrificial significance. The excision of this sacrificial significance even constitutes a grave danger to the Supper if it is not regarded as a loss, if the feeling aroused is that of relief rather than that of hope, hope of the recovery of this sacrificial significance, purified, restored to its true dimensions, freed from culpable exaggeration.

The Reformers asked the Western Church to proceed to the excommunication of the sacrificial aspect of the Supper because its behaviour was such as called for chastisement. The Western Church in its entirety did not agree to this condemnation—whence its division. It seems to me that the moment has arrived—since everything suggests that that particular aspect of eucharistic theology shows signs of a genuine desire for repentance and because it would be shocking to get accustomed to its exclusion—to ask the Reformed Church to re-examine the question whether she is still today set on saying about the Roman Catholic Mass what she said about the medieval Mass in the sixteenth century, that it is "an abominable idolatry",[48] and to make this inquiry publicly, openly and in a brotherly spirit. For so long as this is not done, we Protestants are committed to taking the Mass for what we were obliged to say about it in the sixteenth century.

Now if we continue to describe it in these terms, do we not find ourselves in open contradiction with today's realities, consequently committed to a fight against a foe almost as illusory as Don Quixote's windmills? And if we just stop saying this without the decision not to say it any more, are we not lacking in frankness and courage which are needed to make us valid ecumenical partners with the Roman Catholics?[49] I find the New Testament terminology as well as the patristic unanimity too overwhelmingly in favour of the centrality of the sacrificial theme in a balanced eucharistic theology for me to be able to admit that the recognition of this fact means compromising with the blasphemous abuses of the Middle Ages. I am, too, certain that the Roman Catholics are not yet completely liberated from these abuses not to be convinced that we could best help them to get rid of them by daring to assert by an official pronouncement—but what has happened to the magisterium which we knew in the sixteenth century?—that since the Eucharist is a sacrament of the sacrifice of Christ and a channel of the Church's sacrifice, it must also be interpreted in sacrificial categories.

NOTES

[1] We here confront a classic example of the atrophy which, in protestant theology, has gradually overtaken the themes which did not enter into the polemic against Rome. Indeed, according to protestant theology of the sixteenth and seventeenth centuries, with its emphasis upon fidelity to the patristic tradition,

the polemic against the medieval interpretation—at least as it was then under-stood—of the sacrificial nature of the Eucharist has not removed an idea of the Supper which is very similar to the one I am trying to describe here.

[2] In this first part of the chapter I am leaving aside the sacrificial terminology used in the New Testament with reference to the Eucharist.

[3] The debate on the meaning of ἐστίν seems to me out-of-date, because it has proved impossible to get behind the Greek ἐστὶν, which is universally attested (at least for the bread), to the original Semitic words used by Jesus.

[4] p. 108 f.

[5] Moffat translates πνευματικόν by "supernatural".

[6] Which is clearly the meaning of καθ' ἡμέραν in Matthew 26: 55 for example.

[7] *Petit traité de la sainte cène*, p. 122.

[8] H. Lietzmann is of the opinion that this formula is a quotation from the Antioch eucharistic liturgy, *op. cit.*, p. 257.

[9] "Accedit verbum ad elementum et fit sacramentum". Augustine (*In Evangelium Johannis*, Tr. 80. 3: MPL xxxv 1840).

[10] ... "verbo Dei fiunt, quae antea non fuerunt, sacramenta. Consecrantur enim verbo, et sanctificata esse ostendunt ab eo qui instituit" (W. Niesel, *op. cit.*, p. 260.)

[11] E.g. Matt. 9: 29; 20: 34; Mark 7: 33; Luke 7: 14; cf. Matt. 8: 15; 9: 25; Mark 8: 22; 10: 13, etc.

[12] I dare not venture upon a reasoned appreciation of the interpretation of the eucharistic happening by the help of the doctrine of transubstantiation. I will remark only that, by and large, this doctrine seems to attempt to express and safeguard the reality of the presence of Christ in the bread and wine by a method which oversteps the limits set for theological investigation. It reminds me of what Moses might have related if he had disobeyed the order to stop and adore, and if he had carried out his intention to go round the burning bush to inspect it *from behind*. The recent writings of the best Roman Catholic theologians on this matter, the Conciliar Constitution on Liturgy, seem, however, to con-tradict the opinion generally held in my Church on this question and to facilitate a resumption of the dialogue.

[13] Cf. *Apol.* I, 66. 2; *Dialogue* 70. 4.

[14] Cf. *Adv. Haer.* IV. 18; V. 2.

[15] Speaking of the Gospel ministry, St. Paul sees in it an excessive "hyperbolic power" (ὑπερβολὴ τῆς δυνάμεως, 2 Cor. 4: 7) which must be linked to God, not to the minister. He adds that the trials of the ministry are there to deliver ministers from the temptation to claim possession of this power for themselves and to deliver laymen from the temptation to mistake the minister for the Lord who has called him (cf. Acts 3: 5 ff.; 14: 1–18), but this does not weaken the ὑπερβολὴ τῆς δυνάμεως.

[16] It would be useful to look for the reasons why the rejection, in the "Con-stantinian" tradition of the Church, of the idea of the validity of the sacrament *ex opere operantis* did not have the same consequences for Baptism as it did for the Supper, and why the Supper remained linked to the normal ministry, whereas Baptism was not necessarily so linked. It is one of the aspects of that divergence, which we have already encountered, between baptismal and eucharistic theology

and discipline, a divergence which has had deplorable results both for Baptism and the Supper.

[17] *Op. cit.*, p. 113.

[18] Ἀναξίως I Cor. 11: 27, doubtless means "in a false, distorted way" rather than "unworthily" in the moral sense of the word.

[19] P. Neuenzeit establishes a relationship between 1 Cor. 16: 22 and 1 Cor. 11: 26 ff.; he raises the question whether the same problem does not occur in Heb. 6: 4 ff.; 10: 29; (*op. cit.*, p. 122).

[20] Was Judas present at the institution of the Supper and did he take part in it? Clearly Matthew and Mark locate the announcement of the betrayal, the "woe" to him who betrays the Son of Man and the indication of the betrayer *before* the institution of the Supper (Matt. 26: 23 ff.; Mark 14: 20 ff.) whereas Luke speaks of it *after* (22: 21 ff.). For Matthew and Mark it seems probable then that Judas was excommunicated *before* the institution of the Supper, whereas on Luke's view he had received the communion. Was this why Luke did not report the suicide of Judas (as did Matthew 27: 3 ff.) but states that sudden death struck him as a judgment from God (Acts 1: 18)?

[21] *Ein Sermon von dem neuen Testament d.i. von der heiligen Messe*, Ed. Clémen, I, p. 304.

[22] *Discours catéchétiques* 37, 2–3, quoted by J. M. R. Tillard, *op. cit.*, p. 129.

[23] *Apostolic Constitutions*, VIII, 14. 2.

[24] John 3: 14; 8: 28; 12: 32, 34.

[25] Heb. 9: 11–14; cf. 7: 26; 8: 1 ff.; 10: 19.

[26] Rom. 8: 34; cf. Heb. 7: 25; 9: 24.

[26a] *An Introduction to the Theology of the New Testament*, 1958, pp. 380 f.

[27] A problem which is parallel but opposite is that of the solitary position taken up by Rome on the interpretation of the rôle of Peter and of a Petrine succession.

[28] Rom. 6: 10; Heb. 7: 27; 9: 12, 26 ff.; 1 Pet. 3: 18; cf. Heb. 10: 10, etc. See also on this subject A. Richardson who supports the protests of the Reformers against "the utterly unbiblical (and unpatristic) notion of the Mass as a re-enactment or even a repetition of the sacrifice of Calvary, in which the priest offers afresh the body and blood of Christ as a sacrifice on behalf of the living and the dead" (*op. cit.*, p. 382). It can be stated then that the relation between the uniqueness of the Cross and the Supper is the same as the relation between the uniqueness of the Parousia and the Supper. If it is admitted—as is more generally done—that there is a true and efficacious prefiguration of the Parousia at the time of the Supper, why not admit that there is a true and efficacious "postfiguration" of the Cross at the time of the Supper? The possibility of establishing a living, active link between the unique Cross of Christ and the manifold Eucharists is of the same order as the possibility of establishing a living active link between the unique Parousia of Christ and the manifold Eucharists.

[29] "L'Institution de l'Eucharistie", *Exégèse et Théologie*, Paris, 1961, I, p. 231.

[30] J. Jeremias has established in detail that σῶμα (Paul, Synoptics) or σάρξ (John, Ignatius, Justin) on the one hand, αἷμα on the other, are not anthropological terms but sacrificial (*op. cit.*, pp. 191 f.; 213 ff.). Morever the very verbs which relate what becomes of the body (διδόμενον) and of the blood (ἐκχυννόμενον) come from the language of sacrifice.

[31] τὸ αἷμα τῆς διαθήκης (Matthew, Mark) is a textual echo of Exod. 24: 8 LXX. After erecting an altar, and setting up twelve stones to represent the Twelve Tribes (Is there an inevitable parallel here to the Twelve with whom Jesus instituted the Supper?), offering burnt offerings and pouring half of the blood on the altar, Moses sprinkles the people and reads to them from the Book of the Covenant. In the Supper the blood is linked, not with the crucifixion of Jesus, but with other sacrifices, since the crucifixion was a bloodless sacrifice, the throats of the victims not being cut.

[32] The sacrificial (or at least ritual) co-efficient of the verb ποιεῖν (cf. Exod. 29: 35; Num. 15: 11 ff.; Deut. 25: 9 LXX) is underlined by A. Richardson op. cit., p. 370; J. Jeremias, op. cit., p. 240, etc. M. Goguel in L'Eucharistie des origines à Justin Martyr, Paris, 1910, p. 273, translates ποιεῖν by "celebrate".

[33] When we spoke earlier of the eucharistic species, we saw that Christ's choice of bread and wine was doubtless conditioned by the Judaism with which He identified Himself at His incarnation and within which He makes a meeting-place for all men, to reveal His love to them in the offer of salvation. The very existence of a sacrament of anamnesis likewise links the Church to the Judaism of Jesus; it is only in this Jewish setting that the Supper can be understood. Perhaps this was why the Supper so soon became an offence to men.

[34] Sacrificial terminology applied to the Supper is not of necessity dangerous, since the Church no longer has to deal existentially with pagan sacrifices, but only with the Old Testament. But for that reason the Old Testament, with its blend of nearness and distance which characterizes its Christian interpretation, must live in her heart.

[35] Here is seen again that close link between John 13: 1–20 (where Jesus loves His own εἰς τέλος) and the institution of the Supper.

[36] "Hoc est sacrificium christianorum: multi unum in Christo" (De civitate Dei, x. 6).

[37] "Ubi ei demonstratur, quod in ea re quam offert, ipsa offeratur" (ibid.).

[38] Matt. 10: 38 and par.; Mark 8: 34 and par.

[39] 2 Cor. 1: 5; cf. 2 Cor. 4: 10, etc.

[40] Cf. Rom. 15: 16; Acts 10: 13 ff.

[41] Cf. Phil. 2: 7; 2 Tim. 4: 6; 1 Pet. 1: 2; Rev. 6: 9, etc.

[42] Rom. 12: 1; cf. Eph. 5: 2.

[43] It was Luther, I believe, with the racy strength of his metaphors, who compared the Ascension of Christ and His priestly entry into the heavenly sanctuary (cf. Heb. 9: 11 ff.) to a birth. During childbirth the most difficult moment is the passage of the head. Once the head has emerged, the body follows. But this head must have a body, there must be an ontological link between Christ and the Church, otherwise she would not be able to profit from the Ascension of Christ.

[44] There is an echo here of the nuptial metaphor found in Chapter III; it is the moment, when the Church, the Bride, is presented as an offering, attuned to the One who alone can give her fulfilment when He receives her (παριστάναι, ἁρμόζεσθαι, 2 Cor. 11: 2).

[45] Is this to say the aspect of eschatological joy is the greatest of the three?

[46] One must add that this protest has been so far-reaching that Protestants have more and more lost sight of the fact that in biblical theology propitiation

52109

is not the sole purpose of sacrifice. This has led in Protestantism to a progressive elimination of all sacrificial significance in the Supper.

[47] Which would confirm the fact that in 1 Cor. 11: 22, St. Paul is protesting solely against an Agape divorced from its cultic setting, and by separating the Supper from the Agape, is protecting eucharistic worship against an eschatological effervescence which ignores the fact that the Kingdom of God has not yet been established.

[48] ". . . ein vermaledeyte Abgötterey" (*Heidelberg Catechism*, question 80).

[49] I am very fearful of the re-introduction into our Church of a sacrificial interpretation of the Supper without an open statement of what is being done. To take the Church by surprise is certainly not an act of love towards her. It may be that, in the world, truth sometimes has to be smuggled in (Think of the wonderful complicity of Mary on the day of the Annunciation!). In the Church doors must be flung wide open to truth.

V

PRAYER AND FULFILMENT

THE THESIS I should like to support in this chapter is that the Supper epitomizes the prayer which the Church addresses to God in the name of Jesus Christ; but it is also the résumé of what God is doing in the world at this present moment to fulfil this prayer. In the Supper, the Church's prayer and God's answer to it are expressed and come together.

The history of Christian prayer enables us to advance the idea that the Supper is at one and the same time the centre, the norm and the culminating moment.

The Supper is first of all the centre: from the celebration of the Supper, and especially from the thanksgiving which accompanied and vindicated the fact that Jesus *took* bread and wine,[1] the great Christian liturgical tradition derived its origin and slowly became fixed. To make the Church unlearn the art of prayer, to render her prayers futile, or to make them cease altogether, all one would have to do would be to remove the Supper from the Church's life, either by transferring it to a realm to which Christian people do not have access or by making the celebration of it infrequent. If, on the other hand, one wants to teach the Church anew to make her life one of prayer, one is most likely to succeed by restoring to the Church the full significance of the Supper. History shows that the Eucharist is so powerful a centre of prayer that what issues from it should be directed into an ordered channel within the Church's own freedom to formulate her prayers. But the Supper is even more important for the prayer-life of the Church; to the Supper are brought to be consecrated prayers originating elsewhere and it is in so far as they can be integrated into the Sunday liturgy that they are justified and have their right place. I am referring to the offices, but also to so many other prayers, especially the graces we ask on our meals.

The Supper also supplies the norm for the Church's prayers; it is in the degree to which they are consonant with the Eucharist that they are specifically Christian. This essay is not the place for a theology of prayer; I must be content with the following observations.

Besides the Lord's Prayer, the *Maranatha*, certain doxologies, etc., the New Testament has preserved the text of one prayer, the contents and movement of which are specifically Christian. It is that offered when Peter and John had rejoined the Jerusalem Church after their appearance before the Sanhedrin (Acts 4: 24-30). It consists of two sections: a "preface" which reminds God of what He has done to create and to save the world (v. 24-29) and an act of intercession that the history of salvation might be continued, that the Church should be integrated into this history and that she might participate in its completion. It is then a prayer whose basic purpose is God's plan and its realization in the history of the world. Thy Kingdom come!

What strikes one when taking stock of the prayers of the early Church is the important place that Christian hope plays in them. In short, the Church is asking for the fulfilment of the promises of Christ, and it is in reference to this basic prayer that the other prayers are composed. This is also why the Lord's Prayer which, in its entirety, is a plea for the Kingdom of God, is so clearly the Christian prayer *par excellence*, whether or not in the earliest days it was used at the eucharistic celebration.

Now this expectation of the Parousia which characterizes Christian prayer animated by the eucharistic celebration also becomes the noblest expression of Christian catechesis. To learn to pray as a Christian is to learn to understand as a Christian, to penetrate deeper and deeper into the knowledge of what God is, of what His will is, of what He does. The Eucharist, the school of prayer, is by this very fact the school of faith. Here, too, one can advance the view that to uproot catechetical teaching from the eucharistic soil results either in making faith futile or causing it to wither, for it is by and in the eucharistic celebration that believers learn to meet God and to encounter the world. Christian theology, christology, pneumatology, anthropology and cosmogony are inconceivable, in their elaboration, except in the context of the eucharistic celebration. That is something which experts in the history of dogma do not sufficiently stress.

But the Supper is chiefly the culminating act in the Church's prayer. It is in the Supper that she presents herself in Christ before God and addresses God in the name of Christ. It is here by her prayers she adores God; confesses and celebrates what He has wrought; here that she begs to be integrated into the history of salvation and to become a partner with Him in this history; it is here that she prays for the fulfilment of her hopes, that she reaches out towards what has been promised to her. It is here, too, that she learns to take part in the continual intercession of Christ the High Priest for His own and for the world, and that she practises her own priestly office, since her priesthood can only be a participation in Christ's priesthood. It is here that she offers herself as a holy and living sacrifice.

At this point we return to what we have already seen when speaking of the sacrificial nature of the Supper. What will be seen in the following chapter, when we speak of the Supper as Eucharist in the precise sense of that word, can be briefly mentioned. That is why this short list, vital as it is to the understanding of the Supper, is enough to suggest what is to be said on this subject.

The Supper is the centre, norm, and especially the culminating phase of Christian prayer. But one must have the courage to say too that it is its fulfilment, or rather that it is that element of this prayer which can be fulfilled at present, the gift in anticipation of the final fulfilment, the rough sketch and the prefiguration of the Parousia.

The Supper is this proleptic fulfilment because it imparts Christ in whom lies the pledge of all fulfilment, even more, who is Himself the secret fulfilment of every genuine prayer. Indeed, He taught the Church to ask only what He Himself is or what is fulfilled in and through Him. It is in this meaning of fulfilment that one may say with Calvin, "Jesus Christ . . . is offered to us that we may possess Him and in Him the abundance of all the graces that we can desire".[2] This is why the *Maranatha* is so specifically a eucharistic prayer,[3] that Christianity may rightly be called "the religion of the *Maranatha*".[4] "Adesto, adesto, Jesu, bone pontifex, in medio nostri, sicut fuisti in medio discipulorum tuorum", says a Mozarabic epiklesis.[5] Now, if Jesus comes, everything that one hopes for comes too.

But what is the meaning of the claim that the Supper corresponds to that part of Christian prayer which can be answered here below? The answer is supplied by the following five affirmations.

(1) At the time of the Supper, because of Christ's answer to His followers' *Maranatha*, there is an anticipation of the Parousia. This is why the Supper, especially in certain strata of Pauline theology, takes on the quality of judgment, as shown in the previous chapter. This is

why, although the fact has so often been forgotten, the celebration of the Supper in the early Church was understood as a yearning for the coming of the new heaven and the new earth, for the transformation of the ages to take place, not only sacramentally, but historically: "Let grace come and *let this world pass away*!" (ἐλθέτω χάρις καὶ παρελθέτω ὁ κόσμος οὗτος, Didache 10:6). This supplies one of the poles essential to the Christian theology of the world and its history: the present world, distorted by sin, is under judgment, and if it is to be restored to its true nature, to the Kingdom of God, it is at no less a price than radical self-renunciation; its only chance of salvation is to pass with Christ through death in order to experience resurrection. This is why the eucharistic *Maranatha* is in its essence a terrifying prayer offered on behalf of that which has not already passed from death to life. But for those who have already known baptismal resurrection and for that which they have been able to carry with them, through death towards paschal joy, the *Maranatha*, with its proleptic fulfilment in the Eucharist, becomes a regular confirmation of salvation, a slow adaptation to the life of the Kingdom.

(2) The Supper is the realization of the Lord's Prayer, since it enables us to have communion in Christ in whom this prayer is already mysteriously answered. This is to say that at the time of the Supper, because of the presence of Christ, the name of God is hallowed in a unique and incomparable way; there the manifestation of the Kingdom is already apparent;[6] at the Supper the will of God is already accomplished on earth, and, morever, at every Supper the Church surrenders herself to this will and dedicates herself to God; there the Church in this present moment feeds on the bread of eternal life; through the Supper, the Church whose members are reconciled one to another, as is shown by the kiss of peace, receives the forgiveness of sins; through it, temptation is repulsed and the enterprises of the Evil One thwarted. But above all else, it is at the time of the Supper that men, adopted in Christ because their baptism has made them sharers in His death and resurrection, dare to address God as "our Father".

(3) Because of the factors we have stressed, the Supper in some way lifts the Church up into the Coming Kingdom (*sursum corda*), setting her in the resurrection world. On this point Calvin observed: "Not only did He (God) once call us to possess His heavenly Inheritance: but . . . through hope He has already in some way brought us into the possession of it: . . . not only did He promise us life, but He has already transferred us into this life, rescuing us from death." We have already

spoken of this fulfilment in mentioning the fact that Jesus also instituted the Supper so that the messianic feast should be a present reality in this world, since in Him the messianic Bridegroom had already come to summon before him the Bride who was without spot, wrinkle or any such thing, but holy and blameless.

(4) The nature of fulfilment which rightly belongs to the Supper forms the Church into an eschatological people, the new world coming into being in and through her, so that the Supper becomes for the world the very guarantee of its future, already present in its midst despite the imperceptibility and the weaknesses of the Church. The world must indeed be blinded by its own self-righteousness if it fails to understand that the Supper is the guarantee of its own survival, the very presence of what it is waiting for (here is the second pole of the Christian theology of the world and history). It is at this point that one understands afresh the vital, intimate link that exists between the Lord's Day and the Lord's Meal, that one understands too that the Supper imposes a discipline. Just because of the opportunity which it offers to the world, it must be offered in the sincerest purity, as something which is at the same time "wholly other" and yet offered to the world. The eucharistic discipline is not an exercise in facile Pharisaism, but a stern mission of the Church for the world and in the world: the demonstration that the Kingdom has truly come near us, first in Jesus and now, of His will and choice, in the Church which is His body.

(5) Finally, if the Supper is the prayer of the Church, in the sense not only of the offering of prayer but of its fulfilment, it sets us free for the Kingdom which it brings and in which it involves us. For this reason, believers cannot have their prayers answered without themselves becoming agents of this fulfilment, witnesses and bearers of the presence of the Kingdom, the light of the world, and involved in this way of eschatological life which not only distinguishes and reveals them, but which primarily commits them to become what they are even at the risk of having to experience in the world the fate of their Lord.[7]

To sum up, two things result from this participation in the eucharistic communion viewed as fulfilment of the Church's prayers.

First, the difference between the Church and the world is not only on the cognitive level, the Church already knowing what the world as yet knows not or chooses not to know. This difference, because of the sacramental life, touches the very essence of things: the Church *is* other than the world because she is enlightened, because she has savoured the heavenly gift, because she shares in the Holy Spirit, because she has tasted "the goodness of the word of God and the powers of the age to come" (Heb. 6: 5). The Word and Baptism establish her as tomorrow's people, and the Supper unceasingly renews, confirms and enlarges this awareness. The whole sacramental order belongs to the eschatological era; in truth it sets up outposts of this era in the history of this world.

Secondly, the time has not yet come when prayer ceases to be necessary because the fulfilment is too manifest to be sought any longer. Whence the ambiguous situation of the Church, on which O. Cullmann insists afresh: the Kingdom is here, and yet it can be lost again; fulfilment is here, and yet prayer is still indispensable; the Bridegroom has answered the Bride's *Maranatha* and yet this is not yet the time for unbroken communion;[3] the day of the Lord, the *yom Yahweh*, has struck, and yet we still have the Jewish Sabbath and days whose names remind us of pagan deities. It is like the *Magnificat* which sings of the fall of the mighty and the exaltation of the meek as an event which has already occurred, but this song, for the time being has only one hearer and history piles up contradictions of it.

And that is the truth about the Church and her duty: to hold fast in this tension between what she already has and what she still awaits, between what she already is and what she must become, between the fulfilment and the repetition of her prayer, between the Supper as a messianic meal and the Supper as mere ambiguous prefiguration of that meal—without being made proud or idle by what she already has, or grieving or being discouraged as if she had nothing. By her eucharistic prayer, she still calls in the name of the whole world for the coming of God's Kingdom; in the eucharistic fulfilment she experiences already, on behalf of the whole world, the truth and reality of that Kingdom.

NOTES

[1] Εὐλογήσας (for the bread, Matt., Mark) εὐχαριστήσας (for the bread, Lk. for the cup, Matt., Mark).

[2] *Petit traité de la sainte cène*, p. 113.

[3] Did Jesus teach the *Maranatha* (cf. 1 Cor. 16: 22; Rev. 22: 20; Didache 10: 6) in His eucharistic catechesis as the cry which He would answer (which would explain the fact that the Church allowed some time to elapse before translating it), or was it formulated by the Church to bring about the fulfilment of the promise of Jesus to come again to His followers, to be present in the Supper?

[4] E. Schillebeeckx, *Le Christ, sacrement de la rencontre de Dieu*, Lex orandi No. 31, Paris, 1964.

[5] Quoted by H. Lietzmann, *op. cit.*, p. 105.

[6] Certain variants of Luke's text give the reading for the second petition: "let Thy Holy Spirit come upon us and purify us" (ἐλθέτω τὸ πνεῦμα ἅγιον ἐφ' ἡμᾶς καὶ καταρισάτω ἡμᾶς). This epiklesis, if it may justifiably be seen in a eucharistic context, shows how the Supper may anticipate the coming of the Kingdom, before the Parousia, by the outpouring of the Spirit, which makes the Church into an eschatological people.

[7] A. J. B. Higgins rightly stresses that "to partake of this cup is a criterion of readiness to share in His blood, in His suffering" (*op. cit.*, p. 69).

[8] It is easy to understand how, within the very range of Jewish interpretation, the Fathers interpreted the Song of Songs as a kind of eucharistic dialogue.

VI

MASS AND EUCHARIST

WE HAVE ALREADY encountered the daring claim made by P. Neuenzeit, that, in Christian worship, that which becomes "happening" springs not only from the history of salvation, but from the history of the world by virtue of the cosmological significance of worship.[1] This significance comes from the fact that in Christian worship what is commemorated is the offering of Himself by Jesus for the world (John 6: 51).[2] What remains to be seen in this final chapter is that the Supper is the event which sets the tempo of the Church's life in the world. It is from the Supper that she goes forth into the world, it is to the Supper that she returns from the world. Whence the title of this chapter, which takes up two traditional designations of the Supper. We shall begin with brief definitions of these terms and go on to speak of the "pulsation" of the Church in the world, and then of the Supper as the place and the time which are vital in the Christian apostolate.

I am well aware that the origin of the term Mass is problematical and that, consequently, it is not possible to press it too far in the desire to draw a theology from it, for it does not appear to have been adopted for theological reasons, on the foundation of a study dictated by its etymology. Historians are increasingly agreed on seeing in it simply the Roman technical term (*missa = dismissio*) used to denote the termination of a meeting, the dismissal of participants or hearers in the Senate, in the official and legal courts, at the end of the session. The other etymologies—*missa*, the prayer sent up to God, *missa* as the specific act of one *missus*, *missa* as the latinization of the Hebrew *Missah*, sacrifice,[3] etc.—are increasingly being abandoned.

But this does not explain why the term came into use and was adopted. Was it because of the liturgical solemnity of the dismissal of the catechumens, or of the catechumens first and of the communicants later? The expression *missarum solemnia* was in use. Was it because the need was felt for as neutral a term as possible, having no more overtones in itself than "breaking of bread", for example? But in this case the term would have been chosen as the result of a concerted decision and not haphazard. Was it, in spite of everything, because this act of dismissal was motivated by reasons which had a certain theological implication—in the present age it must take place since Christian worship is still intermittent and sporadic, it cannot yet be dispensed with, and consequently it must impose on Christians something else besides worship: mission?

Whatever may be the answer, on the basis of convention rather than exact semantic deduction, I choose this term, mass, as the first pole of what is to be said on this subject. In any event, it implies a movement of dissociation, of departure, which is the very thing I would emphasize. It is the very moment of this implicit description of the worship of the early Church, found in Luke 24: 36–53, where the Risen Lord comes upon His followers, where He is recognized as the Crucified, where He shares their meal, offers them the key to the interpretation of Scripture, and gives them a task in the world for the time when they receive the Holy Spirit, before giving them His blessing and parting from them.

The second term which forms the other pole of this chapter, the Eucharist, goes back as a technical term to the very origins of the Church.[4] It connotes a movement not of dispersion but of gathering together, of assembly, to become an offering of praise for that which God has done in Jesus Christ for the world's salvation, a celebration of the mighty works of God. This interpretation would enable us—as would also the term anamnesis—to deduce all that is to be said about the Supper, showing especially that these works must be celebrated, given back to God in thanksgiving by those who benefit from them, this act of thanksgiving being the very means by which we become sharers in what we are celebrating. But this movement of coming together is not sufficient to celebrate what Christ has done once for all, for His cross is valid and exemplary for always. So it carries with it, in it, the work of the Church, the harvest of her mission. Indeed, since she shares in the apostolate of the Son, through Him she also shares in His offering. This movement corresponds to that of the Seventy who return to Christ to exult in what they were able to do in His name, but who are bidden to rejoice primarily in what Christ Himself has done for them in assuring them of salvation and in casting Satan from the position of authority which he had usurped (Luke 10: 17–20).

Mass and Eucharist. These two words describe the very movement of the Church in the world, the pulsation of her life in history. Everything is distorted if she is satisfied merely with one of the phases of this movement. The Church is neither exclusively mission, nor exclusively worship; she is mission and worship, and if she turns to the world to teach men the love of God, it is in order to draw the world with her in celebration of this love. Mission is not carried out for its own sake, but so that the "catholicity" of God's purpose may become apparent. Thus the missionary movement begins with dispersal and is fulfilled in a coming together, in a return to the point from which it started, enriched by what it has been able to attain. One sows, not for the sake of sowing, but in order to reap; one does not throw the net for the sake of throwing it, but in order to haul it in overflowing with 153 large fishes (John 21: 4–14), that is to say, in full confidence in the completeness of God's will to save. This to-and-fro movement of the Church's mission in the world—and for it to be possible the Church must certainly be not separated from the world, but distinct from it—this movement which swings between Mass and Eucharist, has its links with history itself and thus with space and time.

When reading the New Testament one is struck by the fact that the missionaries were not content to disperse from one particular place; they came back to their point of departure to render an account, to garner the harvest which had been reaped. The Seventy left Jesus to come back to Him (Luke 10: 1–2, 17–20). Barnabas and Paul left Antioch, and their mission reached its fulfilment at the moment of their return to that city (Acts 13 and 14). For St. Paul, Jerusalem was the centre from which he went out and to which he returned during the first phase of his missionary activity (cf. Rom. 15: 19, 25 ff.), and the collection which he took to Jerusalem, and which at the risk of his life he wished to take himself, was, as it were, his own Eucharist and that of the pagans whom he had won for the faith (he actually called it this in 2 Cor. 9: 11 f.). This first lap accomplished,[5] he intended to make the capital of κύριος Καῖσαρ the point of departure and return in a new phase of his proclamation of κύριος Χριστός (Rom. 15: 23 ff.). One may even wonder whether the way the Acts opens (1: 1–11), speaking of the commissioning of the disciples, of the restoration of Israel and of the return of Christ (to Jerusalem, too, without doubt), does not make Jerusalem the departure-point and the arrival-point of the Church's apostolate in the world—notwithstanding the different geographical and historical "cycles", which were complementary to but dominated by this overall apostolic "cycle" and integrated into it.[6] This would mean that those who were charged with the task of gathering together the messianic nation remained responsible for it until the Parousia. From this fact sprang the obligation for them to transmit their mission to others if it was not fulfilled at the time of their death.[7]

Within this great apostolic-eucharistic cycle, the Holy Table, which establishes the local Church as an earthly sacrament of the heavenly Jerusalem, supplies a similar centre from which the Church can go out and to which she can return. It is from there—from this anamnesis of the whole history of salvation and its culmination in Jesus of Nazareth, from this "ecclesial" awareness, from this communion with the Risen Christ and with men who have become brothers, from this life-giving meal, from this secret fulfilment of every prayer—that the Church enters into the world, there to be salt and light, to sanctify and to protect it, there to be the witness of the love and forgiveness of God by knowing herself how to love and pardon.

It is in this sense that the Supper is missionary: from the Supper, the Church is sent into the world to bear the sufferings and the glory of Christ because she is His Body and His Bride. Thus it is not the celebration in itself which is missionary. This is reserved—at least in the very wise view of the ancient Church—for the baptized alone, for what takes place there would seem foolish and scandalous in the eyes of the world. It takes place behind closed doors, as at the time of its institution before, or at the time of its ratification after, the passion and glorification of Jesus. The desire to make of the Supper a missionary action seems to me to change the content of the Supper and to transform it into a *verbum visibile*, into a spectacle which no longer involves in communion those who are present. But if the Holy Table is the place from which the Church is sent out into the world, it is also the place to which she returns from the world, laden with her harvest like the disciples after the miraculous draught of fish, or like Israel coming back to the Promised Land after the hard struggles of the Exodus or returning after the Exile.

This, then, is the Eucharist: the weekly sacrificial pilgrimage in which the Church, like the servants in the parable, enters into the joy of the returning Lord, offering Him, with herself, all that has resulted for Him from what had been lent to her, rejoicing in Him for all the gifts unceasingly bestowed by the salvation He has won for the world once for all, and celebrating the strength and welcoming power of this salvation. Thus the Eucharist establishes the Church in her catholicity as the Mass had established her in her apostolicity. For this reason the Eucharist can never be other than a festival, however great may be the misery, the sadness, the despair of the world from which she withdraws to celebrate the gift of salvation. The Church need have no problem here if she remembers that a Christian festival bears no resemblance to an orgiastic celebration (cf. Matt. 26: 6–13 and par.).

This pulsation in which the Mass and the Eucharist start from and come back to the same Table is found also in time. At the centre of the great chronological cycle of the history of salvation which runs from the resurrection of Christ to His return (parallel to the geographical cycle mentioned above), a theology of Sunday must be developed, since it is from Sunday and until Sunday that the Church lives out her days. Attention was drawn earlier to the importance of the fact that the anamnesis of the death of Christ was not originally celebrated on the night when He was betrayed nor on the day when He was crucified, but on the day of His resurrection. W. Rordorf has advanced cogently the hypothesis according to which "the first day of the week" (Matt. 28: 1; Mark 16: 2, 9; Luke 24: 1; John 20: 1; Acts 20: 7; 1 Cor. 16: 2) took on the name "the Lord's day" (Rev. 1: 10), κυριακὴ ἡμέρα because it was the day of the Lord's *meal*, κυριακὸν δεῖπνον,[8] which implies that in the very early days of the Church the Supper was celebrated every Sunday, but only on Sundays.[9] But Sunday is also called the eighth day—for the first time in the Epistle of Barnabas (15: 8).[10] This expression never became the current designation for Sunday despite the theological importance it had in the early Church. All the same, it suggests that if Sunday is not just the first, but still more the eighth day of the week, it is not simply because the anamnesis of the past victory of Christ was commemorated on that day, but because already "the beginning of another world" (Barnabas 15: 9) was sensed, for the eighth day "is the age to come" as St. Irenaeus said (*Adv. haer.* 5: 28, 3). Because of the Supper, Sunday is the day of the week in which the resurrection of Christ and the prefiguration of the resurrection of the whole cosmos come together. The resurrection of Christ is the pledge of cosmic resurrection. It is the day when the Church sets out in its mission of announcing to the world the victory of Christ and the day which prefigures the acceptance of the world into the manifest brilliancy of that victory, the ἀνάπαυσις, the day of true rest.

NOTES

[1] *Op. cit.*, p. 229.

[2] Cf. 6: 33.

[3] An etymology proposed or often defended by Lutherans in the sixteenth century—cf. Y. Brilioth, *op. cit.*, p. 251.

[4] Didache 9 and 10; see also the use of the verb εὐχαριστεῖν in the accounts of the institution of the Supper (Matt. 26: 27; Mark 14: 23; Luke 22: 19; 1 Cor. 11: 24).

[5] Undoubtedly one must interpret the cycle, the κύκλος of Rom. 15: 19 as meaning that Paul left Jerusalem with the intention of returning.

[6] It is the Church rather than the Jewish people who, under the New Covenant, must return to Jerusalem, as the return of the Jews to Jerusalem has no direct bearing on the history of salvation, although obviously it has an indirect bearing. It enables them to be re-organized politically, to make decisions, including theological decisions, as a nation, to be present, at least in the person of their ambassadors, in all the countries of the world, including those in which they were not dispersed—which is of vital importance for the *Christian* mission.

[7] We have already seen the importance of the "apostolic succession" for the Eucharist; it is equally vital for the apostolate, so vital that you cannot deprive the evangelical ministry of its missionary dimension and responsibility. One could go so far as to say that only those who fulfil their apostolate can also minister at the Eucharist. If one were to introduce this missionary dimension into the grim ecumenical debates on the apostolic succession, there would be an easing of tension because the balance would be restored. It was to the *same* men that Jesus said, "Do this in memory of me", and "Go and teach all nations, baptizing them . . ." In other words, a bishop or a pastor has the right of presiding over the Eucharist of his Church only if he also leads in the carrying out of her "Mass".

[8] *Sunday*, 1968, pp. 201 f., 220 f. W. Rordorf observes on this point that it is wrong to equate Sunday with the Lord's Day when one deprives the day of that which undoubtedly gave it its name, the Lord's meal. The adjective κυριακός in the New Testament is found only joined to ἡμέρα or δεῖπνον.

[9] This is the opinion of the majority of liturgiologists. For the theology of the Eucharist, a history of the frequency of the Supper in the early Church, made jointly by historians from different denominations, would be extremely interesting. Indeed, perhaps only such a history could record, with the highest perceptivity, the development and the emphases, even the distortions of eucharistic theology.

[10] Possibly also in Slavonic Enoch 33: 1 f.

CONCLUSION

After attempting to understand the Supper and its rightful place in the life of the Church, I shall stress just two brief conclusions.

The first concerns the Supper as a sacrament of Christian unity. One is well aware of all the problems which this raises, since eucharistic communion is the seal of the union of the Churches and since Christian division, in the situation where it is not conjured away or sidestepped, is most evident in the fact that it is impossible to take communion together.[1] How then can one speak of the Supper as a sacrament of Christian unity? We must do this by first speaking of the unity of the Supper itself.

In *Eucharistic Faith and Practice*, Y. Brilioth insists on the fact that the Supper is not just made up of thanksgiving, communion, commemoration, sacrifice and mystery, but equally it is the outcome of the unity, simultaneity and balance of all these various phases.[2] In this essay, we have broken down the Supper into six fundamental phases, each one doubly polarized. Now the same conclusion is reached: it is in so far as all these phases are given due consideration, in so far as the Supper is freely allowed to be just what it is without any single one of its component elements being disregarded, made light of or cut out for the benefit of some other element, that it will be the vital sacrament of ecclesial communion. In other words, if in the divided Church the Supper is again to become the factor and motive of unity which it really is, then it must be allowed to recover the fullness and the balance of its unity. And this must happen in each Church; when it does it will bring about a radical reform in each of them.

Consequently, the first task facing the separated Churches on this issue is for each of them to rediscover for herself the meaning of the Eucharist and to give it the place which belongs to it. Such a rediscovery obviously will not come about without a regular exchange of information, results of research, experiences, cautions, criticisms and encouragement, nor without periodically putting to the test the things which still seem to separate the Churches in this matter to see whether the reasons for separation are still valid or whether they are becoming less relevant or disappearing altogether. Such a rediscovery will never happen within the context of a single denomination; but it is at the centre of its own life that each Church must rediscover eucharistic joy, starting from the Supper as she celebrates it, and, once this rediscovery has happened, that is to say when in each Church the Supper has regained a unity which takes fully into account the diversity of its components, there will actually be no need for unity between the different Churches to be brought about: it can be affirmed as a fact and will only need to be organized.[3]

My second conclusion is: the eucharistic event must be distinguished from the eucharistic theology and celebration. In other words, one must attribute to the eucharistic event a virtue which derives, not from the way (which is expressed so falteringly) in which it is interpreted, nor from the manner (so far short of the joy which should characterize it) in which it is celebrated, but from its institution by Christ and its quickening by the Holy Spirit. This means that the Supper is a sacrament of faith. This in no sense implies that its action is restricted to those who believe. Otherwise it would not carry that aspect of judgment emphasized at the close of what the Apostle says in 1 Corinthians 11: 30 ff. On this issue, the Supper is comparable to the apostolic ministry which is "the aroma of Christ to God among those who are being saved and among those who are perishing, to one a fragrance from death to death, to the other a fragrance from life to life" (2 Cor. 2: 15 f.).

To say that the Supper is a sacrament of faith is to say that before he can discern the body of Christ therein the communicant needs the intervention of God and his own acceptance of this intervention. For what could be more peculiar than to claim that in this piece of bread, in this sip of wine, are gathered together all the things we have listed, if it were not for one thing only which establishes and justifies this claim: that in the man Jesus of Nazareth "the whole fullness of deity dwells bodily" (Col. 2: 9)? One finds oneself at the very focal point of the election by God of that which is foolish and weak to confound that which, in this world, is wise and strong.

This is why the Supper demands a catechesis—as is shown by the hard word, which was nevertheless the word of eternal life, spoken by Jesus when He explained the Bread of Life (John 6: 51–60). This is why the Supper demands the discernment of what is taking place; this is why access to the Table is not open to all comers. In one of his homilies on St. Matthew, St. Chrysostom cries:

> Let us obey God in everything; let us never disobey Him—even if what He says seems contrary to reason and to our intelligence. Do we not act in the same way in the celebration of the mysteries where we do not take account only of what strikes our senses, but where we retain its words? Now His word cannot deceive us.[4]

Such expressions are often found in the Fathers when they try to sum up in words the very mystery of the communion which operates between the symbols of the body and blood of Christ and the communicant. So they frequently have recourse (following 1 Cor. 10: 2), to the adjective spiritual, pneumatic (in contrast to carnal, fleshly) to emphasize that what takes place at this time is transfigured by the work of the Holy Spirit, who brings it about that when one eats this flesh and drinks this blood one is brought into the very forward movement of the history of salvation and laid open to the life eternal which Jesus gives as He gives Himself.

The acknowledgment of the spiritual virtue of the Eucharist is as scandalous (in the biblical sense) as the acknowledgment that all the fullness of God dwells in Jesus; it does not arise from our human heart, it is given to us, and it is in faith that we can receive it. Thus it demands from the man who makes this acknowledgment an act of self-renunciation and of confidence in Christ, whose word then becomes more important than anything we ourselves might have said about this bread which is broken and shared, about this cup which is lifted up and distributed.

> The communication which we have in the body and blood of the Lord Jesus . . . is a spiritual mystery, which cannot be seen with the eye, nor understood by the human intelligence. So it is depicted for us by visible signs . . . in such a way, however, that it is not a stark figure but clothed with its truth and substance.[5]

The Supper as the anamnesis of the reconciling death of Christ and as the invocation of the Holy Spirit to fulfil its true purpose, the Supper as ecclesial revelation, the Supper as an act of nuptial and fraternal communion, the Supper as sacrifice and Bread of Life, the Supper as the place and moment when the Church's prayer and God's answer meet, the Supper as the heart which beats at the centre of the life of the Church in the world: it is impossible to speak of it thus without *believing* what Jesus said when He purposed the Supper and when He explained it. Where we speak of it in this way, we can understand that Christians of olden days preferred to be arrested rather than to renounce the Supper, and with the martyrs of Abitina we learn to say: "Sine Domenico (scil. convivio esse) non possumus": we cannot live without the Lord's meal.[6]

NOTES

[1] We have seen in Chapter III that, whatever merits it may possess, intercommunion can never solve the problem of Christian division, since it maintains the different confessional Churches in their division.

[2] *Op. cit.*, pp. 14 ff.

[3] Perhaps the "catholics" will protest at this by emphasizing that no Church by herself is in a position to rediscover, starting from the Supper as she celebrates it, the eucharistic fullness, and consequently the pledge and opportunity of its ecclesial fullness, because in the situation where the sacrament of ordination is lacking "the authentic and integral substance of the eucharistic mystery cannot possibly have been preserved"—to use the words of the conciliar decree *De Oecumenismo* (no. 22). This is the obstacle one is always coming up against in ecumenical discussions and it must be faced for good and all without evasion. Until proof to the contrary is supplied by "protestants", this obstacle does not seem to me to be unsurmountable. In fact, if it is clear that to preside over the Eucharist one must be authorized by Christ, if this authorization is fitted into the apostolic succession, and if this authorization is ordinarily conveyed by the laying on of hands, it is not obvious that this ministry, essential as it is to the Church if it is to be the Church, is necessarily tied to any one of its sociological forms e.g. episcopacy of the diocesan type (eventually the presbyterate validated by its sharing in the episcopacy). But that is something which our Church ought to state and support with serious historical arguments instead of so often making fun of those who suspect our churchmanship and who often do so simply because we have not had the knowledge, the desire, the courage to reply to their doubts otherwise than by bringing up our doubts on their position. This is not to say that, once our ministry has been recognized as essentially valid, we do not have to agree to a very serious sociological readjustment of its nature. Could the "catholic" Churches not help us? "The Catholic Church", affirms Ghislain Lafont, "cannot recognize a Reformed community as being any more a Church than this community consents to be a Church" ("L'appartenance fondamentale à l'Eglise", in M. J. Le Guillou and Gh. Lafont, *L'Eglise en marche*, Cahiers de la Pierre-qui-vire, no 23, Paris, 1964, p. 85). And why not? Should we not walk two miles with the one who expects us to go only one mile with him (Matt. 5: 41)? Would not the most brotherly service be for the "catholic" Churches to recognize us for a Church more than we take ourselves for such? This would compel us to say whether we are effectively as much a Church as they would claim we are, and to prove it by really becoming a Church.

[4] Quoted by Paul VI in the Encyclical *Mysterium fidei* (*loc. cit.*, pp. 756 f.).

[5] J. Calvin, *op. cit.*, p. 111.

[6] Quoted by J. A. Jungmann, *La Liturgie des premiers siècles*, p. 27.